pg 111
18 12

⌣ ⌣

ANAPEST

⌣ ⌣ —

Some Jazz a While

DACTYLIC

⌣ ⌣

Yet,
BE CAREFUL —
PARADOXICALLY —
REASON DOESN'T EQUAL TRUTH
69

community

(
Reason
(questioning
societal
truths)   < versus >

loss is an apology

< PERVERTS >

Some Jazz a While
COLLECTED POEMS

Miller Williams

University of Illinois Press
Urbana and Chicago

© 1999 by Miller Williams
Manufactured in the United States of America
1 2 3 4 5 C P 5 4 3 2 1

This book is printed on acid-free paper.

Library of Congress Cataloging-in-Publication Data
Williams, Miller.
Some jazz a while : collected poems / Miller Williams.
p.   cm.
ISBN 0-252-02463-X (acid-free paper)
ISBN 0-252-06774-6 (pbk. : acid-free paper)
I. Title.
PS3545.I53352A17   1999
811'.54—ddc21   98-25476
CIP

For Jordan
and for Lucinda, Robert, and Karyn,
and Rebecca, Sarah, Sam, Charles, Emily, and Reuben

In memory of
John Ciardi, Howard Nemerov, and Flannery O'Connor
my friends, my teachers

* rhyme makes poetic argument *

* loyal opposition *

"ON THE WAY HOME"
(SESTINA

"A NOTE TO GOD" p 9
"FOR JORDAN" p. 44 - Villanelle
"Vision + prayer" p48 - refrain
"In the Beg." p12
"WHY GOD" p 68
"NOTES 73
"ART PHOTO" 177
"ENTROPY" 136
"FOR WUNDA" 134 7 villanelle
"were" - iambic + fierace
"Holiday Inn" 228
"God" 256
"of HISTORY + HOPE" 259
"WAKING FROM A DREAM" 270

Contents

Some Jazz a While

From *A Circle of Stone*

Funeral

He pulled off on the shoulder, less to lend
respect than room, because the road was narrow
in the rain
and saw the procession creep around the bend
to where his squinting eyes had caught the sign
of the Zion African Methodist Episcopal Church
and an unpronounceable county line.

Three faced three tall men straight and brown
braced against its weight and let it down.

He pulled back onto the road as the rain stopped
and the sun set,
and though that preachers sin and doctors die
was not even now a thing he would have thought of,
he turned to miss a rabbit caught in his lights
and tried awhile to say the name of the county
before he found his speed and checked his watch
and tuned in Memphis for the lightweight fights.

For Lucy, on the Twelfth Month

Here he comes,
still bent against the winds of last October
tasting the air with his lips
like a fish nibbling water,
because he is old and forgets
he is not a fish,

1

who said that time would thicken and grow sour
when these rings had held a year together,
when the alchemy had spent its power
and gold became the lead it always was.

Round as most round things
and important as death,
who built a narrow bed in this strange meadow,
when the grass grows brown
till getting up undoes the lying down,
when long-tongued truth has killed the quiet liar
and this wet war gives way to a dusty peace,
ask him in and offer him a glass.
Let him say the things that he was saying.
Now, for now, go turn the music higher.
Let the long decrease of love
find us playing.

The Associate Professor Delivers an Exhortation to His Failing Students

Now when the frogs
that gave their lives for nothing
are washed from the brains and pans
we laid them in,
I leave to you,
who most excusably misunderstand,
the margins of my talks,
which because I am wise
and am a coward
were not appended to the syllabus

but I will fail to tell you
what I tell you
even before you fail to understand
so we might,
in a manner of speaking,
go down together.

2

I should have told you something of importance
to give at least a meaning
to the letter:

how, after hope, it sometimes happens

a girl, anonymous as beer,
telling forgotten things in a cheap bar

how she could have taught here (as well as I.)
Better.

The day I talked about the conduction of currents
I meant to say
be careful about getting hung up in the brain's things
that send you screaming like madmen through the town
or make you
like the man in front of the grocery store
that preaches on Saturday afternoons
a clown.

The day I lectured on adrenalin
I meant to tell you
as you were coming down
slowly out of the hills of certainty

empty your mind of the hopes that held you there.
Make a catechism of all your fears

and say it over.

This is the most of you . . . who knows . . . the best
where God was born
and heaven and confession
and half of love:

from the fear of falling
and being flushed away
to the gulp of the suckhole and that rusting gut
from which no Jonah comes;

that there is no Jesus and no hell;

that God, square root of something equal to all,
will not feel the imbalance when you fall;

that rotting you will lie unbelievably alone
to be sucked up by some insignificant oak
as a child draws milk through straws
to be its bone.

These are the gravity that holds us together
toward our common sun.

Every hope getting out of hand
slings us hopelessly outward one by one
till all that kept us common is undone.

The day you took the test
I would have told you this:
that you had no time to listen for questions
hunting out the answers in your files
is surely the kind of irony
poems are made of;

that all the answers at best are less than half

and you would have remembered
Lazarus
who hung around with God or the devil for days
and nobody asked him

anything.

But if they do,
if one Sunday morning they should ask you
the only thing that matters after all,
tell them the only thing you know is true:

tell them failing is an act of love
because
like sin
it is the [commonality] within;

— everybody fails even the professor -ego -

how failing together we shall finally pass
how to pomp and circumstance all of a class,
noble of eye, blind mares between our knees,
lances ready, we ride to Hercules.

The day I said this had I meant to hope
some impossible punk on a cold slope,
stupidly alone,
would build himself a fire
to make of me an idiot

steal fire from the gods -

Anti - prometheus

and a liar.

For Robert, Son of Man

With eyes that have found the rain and first stars
you looked from your face to my face
Robert . . . son
What are these for?
Your manhood held in your fingers
where frogs and rocks were held
in the wild yards.

Then your great things were boulders coming down
tumbling from some cold and holy place
What are these for?
Loudly through centuries
to find me here in this Buck Rogers town

this year in this Roy Rogers room, with you,
holding my name, looking at my long look
What are these for?
I'm full of lies to tell
to a boy of five, half-Christian and half-Jew.

Rolling from where it tumbled when you spoke
the answer comes ochre and smelling of earth
and we are together
in a circle of stone
where the sun slips red and new
to a stand of oak.

June Twenty, Three Days After

When I was a boy and a man would die
we'd say a verse when the hearse went by
one car two car three car four
someone knocking on the devil's door.

I smoked all night myself awake
and saw the lights and the day break.
When the sun was done with the final star
I left the house and the door ajar
and went to the church. The father was nice
but the holy water was cold as ice.
I found a friend and felt his hand
fall through mine like crumbling sand.
I went to hear the talk in the square
but there were headless people there.
I turned to the clock for the time of day
but the hole in the wall had nothing to say.
Callous of heaven and careless of hell
you knew something you didn't tell.
The soul you said was only fear,
and heaven, well heaven at best was here.
So heaven is gone if that was it
and the soul lies there in the private pit
but hell is big and hell is a bone
and hell comes in from the edge of alone.
Hell is a dead girl who walks through the town
and hunts for my bed to lay herself down.

On the Death of a Middle-Aged Man *die alone*

Beverly
who wished his mother wanting a girl again
had called him something at best ambiguous
like Francis or Marion
went for fifteen years to the Packard plant
and turned for Helen, who punched the proper holes,
the bumperless bodies.

He took her
to dinner once and left her notes in secret
when hair fell down his forehead and refused
the foreman's job.

Except for
sex q
when she was seven her brother which couldn't count
when she was twelve the preacher and that was for God
she never did nothing

Christ would have died for.
Going home
before the coffin was lowered because of the clouds
he fell in front of a car because of the rain.
There were just enough
to (bear) him
counting the foreman a man from the shift a cousin
come to lay claim.

A woman played the piano.   *questioning religion*
(A minister who kept forgetting his name
said he was forgiven|
that he would be forever at the bosom of Abraham
which was the preacher's way of saying heaven.

Original Sin

Wednesday nights
I walked in shadows past prayer meeting lights
and gave my time
for an hour and a half at the movies
and God's dime.

[I was scared]
when the girl who sold the tickets because she was dared
by a man as old
as my father let me feel.
She was cold

and this surprise
was my revelation—but I made lies
and looking at her
twisted my mouth as if it
didn't matter.

In bed my hand
was cold still and the fingers I let pretend
that she was lying
white on a blue hill,
birds flying.

Slowly wrong
I love my wife a time and the night long
I feel the hair
of a high girl grinning red
a night of prayer.

From *So Long at the Fair*

A Note to God Concerning a Point
from an Earlier Communication

Baseball players know the meaning of sacrifice
so did St. Francis
Jesus on the cross
Judas hanged
so do monks keeping their mouths shut forever
nuns sleeping alone.

The choice was easy and the burden light
because the other way was harder than possible.
Nuns are faithful to a husband who is rich
and monks have partnership
in a damned good deal.

That, Sir, is the point.
We invest ourselves always in some Return.
Sacrifice is a way of winning
and we have misnamed it.

But, Sir, I wonder
if there is no way I can deny myself
and everything we give we give in trade
what is sin but witless bargaining
and virtue but a good eye for horses
and a taste for mansions.

Handwritten annotations:
- societal heros
- ⟶ bunt
- ⟶ odd juxtaposition
- vow of silence
- sacrifice is easy
- achieving salvation
- abstract
- calls every action into question —
- criminal = insane
- law = reason
- know there's a payoff

I am aware things are done in mysterious ways
and only ask.

You will call it doubt
but, Sir, you would not believe

how much it seems like the old praise
you would recall from Pentecostal days

a confusion of tongues.

Weatherman

He was always there
a clumsy-grammared hick with a crooked tie
and we turned him on
the way we scrub before meals
and say grace
when no one clearly needs it but in case
of unlikely plagues
the visitation of demons or an evil eye.

We tolerated his talk of a sky not ours
followed his endless scribbling on the wall
because it's best to be if possible
unsurprised by rain.

The hurricane came, was coming
and only that face
transported out of space to the living glass
could tell us how close it was
when it turned hard to the north
and smelled our streets.

10

On that late September afternoon
when even the sky seemed heavy with sandbags
we gathered before the bright box of his knowing,
offered him our faith
pledged to buy Pepsi
commended our homes and children
into his hand.
We were almost sure
by making the marks over the shape of our state
he could conjure wind back from the water,
water from the land.

And when it was gone,
after we dragged the fallen tree away
and cleaned the walk and put the window in,
we were a town
of forty thousand people
who had been a worship
and a fear.
He was a man
who kept a ritual
we suffered him
after the news.

Think Also of Horseshoes

Look at the nails on the wall.
Study the straight line.
Think of the man who hammered them years ago.
He was a serious man with a fanciful wife.

Hear the tailgate bang on the back of a truck.
Think about the man who put it there.
Think of his daughter failing the fifth grade.

Unwrap a cigar.
Think of the man who planted the tobacco.
Think of his dog peeing on the plants.

Turn a rusty bottle cap out of the ground.
Think of the boy who drank the strawberry soda.
Think of him delivering *The Democrat*
chased by the dog run over
today by the truck
made by the man lost in Michigan
whose daughter is misspelling words for a bored teacher
who writes *True Confessions* for the fanciful wife
of the diligent carpenter who is dead now.

In the Beginning

*conceit extended
metaphor?*

In the beginning God began
to turn a field and planted man.

Now God was good and God was wise
as young gods go, and in his eyes

was a time of harvest. So he made
a plow and a hoe and a scythe-blade.

And the arm swung and the seed was sowed
and the back bent and the field was hoed

and the rains of time and the light of law
fell on the land and the farmer saw

that it was good, and he blessed the seed
and cursed the worm and pulled the weed.

The ground broke back. But out of the shoot
there came no flower, there came no fruit.

serpent

Only a worm from under the ground.
He crept across the weeds. The sound

of dead leaves cracking under the weight
of a worm was clear at the farmer's gate.

God talked to Himself like a man in need
of friends, and turned the last good seed

7 couplet

in the cup of his hand that was black and wet
from a farmer's land and a farmer's sweat.

*conceit –
extended
metaphor*

He heard the cells coming awake,
the shell of the seed about to break.

He held it deep in the wrap of his hand
and found a hidden rise of land

*loyal
opposition/*

a black mound near his door
where seed had never been before,

put it there and there he sat,
watched and waited, frowned and spat

on the private place. The thing broke free
like the sun rising out of the sea.

That's the way we came to pass
Christmas, Easter, and the Mass.

*rhyme mocks the
content –
– simplicity*

last good = Jesus

The Caterpillar

Today on the lip of a bowl in the backyard
we watched a caterpillar caught in the circle
of his larval assumptions

My daughter counted
half a dozen times he went around
before rolling back and laughing
I'm a caterpillar, look
she left him
measuring out his slow green way to some place
there must have been a picture of inside him

13

After supper
coming from putting the car up
we stopped to look
figured he crossed the yard
once every hour
and left him
when we went to bed
wrinkling no closer to my landlord's leaves
than when he somehow fell to his private circle

Later I followed
bare feet and door clicks of my daughter
to the yard   the bowl
a milk-white moonlight eye
in the black grass

It died

I said Honey they don't live very long

In bed again
re-covered and re-kissed
she locked her arms and mumbling love to mine
until turning she slipped
into the deep bone-bottomed dish
of sleep

Stumbling drunk around the rim /
I hold
the words she said to me across the dark

I think he thought he was going
in a straight line

And When in Scenes of Glory

When I had been born eight years I was born again
washed in the waters of life
and saved from hell
from the devil the Baptists the Campbellites
and the Pope

When I was told about Santa Claus and the sun
and learned for myself
that trees feel their leaves fall off
and scream at night

I thought about Jesus Christ who had long hair
was hung by the hands
buried and came alive

(in the Roxy Saturday afternoons
rag-dragging zombies came alive in caves
the blood of people made them live forever)

God come down

With hands that could have torn the hills apart
the preacher hammered the tinfoil of my faith
and words came teaching me
out of the terrible whirlwind of his mouth
the taste of evil
bitter and hot as belch
the agony of God
building the gospel word by believable word
out of the wooden syllables of the South

God come down

and over the pews over the dry domes
amens rose up like birds
beating the air for heaven
heading for home and roost
in the right eye

Come for the sake of Jesus

and the white thigh
of Mrs. Someone sitting in the choir

Boy do you believe

Yessir I do

A woman so skinny I could smell her bones
hugged me because I'd turned away from sin

Going home at night after the preaching
after prayers and dinner on the ground
curling in the backseat of the car
I began to feel like a thickening of the dark
almost my mother talking to my father
almost my father singing to himself
my name a gospel song
and a long applause like gravel under the tires

until I heard the wings
and knew it had come
what I had killed and couldn't come anymore
to hunger against the black glass of the car
the thing you think what would happen
if you saw its face

I'd have prayed to God not to have a flat
but God would have laughed
and it would have sounded like
the flapping of wings
over the old Dodge
over the grinding of gravel
and the hymn of grace

Floating with fishes under the river of sound
I remembered with my last dull thought
before I drowned
that I was saved from sin and the world was lost

The river stopped
and the world stopped
and I am lifted up

to be dropped again by my father
onto an unmade bed in a borrowed room
to wait my ankles crossed holding my breath
a dumb kid in some silly game
for the law straining around the earth to crack
and the rock roll back

Monday morning we had oatmeal for breakfast
After school Ward West kicked the piss out of me
Tuesday it snowed

Euglena

Microscopic monster
germ father, founder of the middle way
who first saw fit to join no clan
but claim the best of both
you are more than clever.

Swimming, you go to what meal is.
Green, you make what isn't.

Fence rider,

you've held your own for twenty
million years

who might have been a tulip
or a tiger
you shrewd little bastard.

You Wouldn't Say They Didn't Get Along Exactly

He had loved her
if being in love is believing that you are

but then when the child was being born
he tried to feel love
crawling like amoebas through his veins
and there was nothing
but the guilt of being foreign
to the awful separation of her pains.

Still when they crossed the line
of the first state that was theirs
and not their fathers'
they touched without meaning to
and meant it

and when they pumped at love
and she was softened by the bathroom light
he wanted her that moment for
all time
but she didn't believe it after breakfast.

The Widow

The Hammond organ lubricates the air.
The kind mortician conducts her to her place
of honor. A man with a painted puppet's face
they say is her husband's face is obviously there

in front of her. She would have the casket
closed, but his sister would not. The minister cries
how gloriously the man is dead who lies
before him daily with a face like plastic,

prays that God who took him out of order
will keep his soul from torment, will adorn him
with a crown of stars, will hold with those that mourn him.
It is not hard, she thinks, but it will be harder.

The wail of the Hammond weakens, her mind goes black,
turning quickly out of the moment meanders
on curious ways. She looks at his nose. She wonders
if they went and slit the good blue suit in the back

Buried in her best [handwritten annotation]

and if his shoes are tied, if he has on
the socks they didn't ask for but she sent,
if they still use pennies, decides of course they don't,
hopes they will have their fill and be done with him soon.

It would not be fair to say she is not grieving. *solitude of self* [handwritten annotation]
She did not want to come, but she is aware
how there will be silence, there will be pleasures to bear
in silence, and dark creatures unbehaving.

Consciousness is power [handwritten annotation]

She did not want to come. She will not be taken
to tears. But she is aware some moment will crush
the brain suddenly, that she will go home and wish
burglars had come there and the blind windows were broken.

Sale

Partnership dissolved. | *solitude* [handwritten annotation]
Everything must be sold.
Individually or the set
as follows:

disintegration of physical self [handwritten annotation]

Brain, one standard, cold.
Geared to glossing.
Given to hard replies.
Convolutions convey the illusion
of exceptional depth.
Damaged.

Think. But you are not thinking.

One pair of eyes. Green. Like new.
Especially good for girls and women walking,
wicker baskets,
paintings by Van Gogh,
red clocks and frogs, chicken snakes and snow.

Look. But you are not looking.

One pair of ears, big. Best offer takes.
Tuned to Bach, Hank Williams, bees,
the Book of Job.
Shutoff for deans, lieutenants, and
salesmen talking.

Listen. But you are not listening.

Mouth, one wide.
Some teeth missing.
Two and a half languages. Adaptable to pipes
and occasional kissing.
Has been broken but in good repair.
Lies.

Tell me. Why can't you tell me?

Hands, right and left.
Feet. Neck. Some hair.
Stomach, heart, spleen and
accessory parts.

Starts tomorrow
what you've been waiting for
and when it's gone

it's gone.

Accident: A Short Story

1

Listening to Billy Graham,
reading my way to a snake farm
live grizzly bear   two-headed cow
    100 yards ahead
I saw the car,
its private parts turned public,
the wheels still spinning,
reeling in the runners from all directions.
I found you mumbling blood to the barbed wire fence,
all of its blackbirds flown,
hubcap at your head like a helmet,
your legs full of ankles.

Between your coontail Buick
and your split woman
telling heaven her minor miseries,
I did what I could, kneeling as if I knew
what the faces ballooning around us thought I knew,
to call an ambulance. Someone ran around
to drop a handkerchief
go in and out the window
find a phone.

2

I looked at my watch because it was late.
Because it was late I cursed you to hell.
She was waiting and round,
she was waiting and young,
but there we were hung
your head in my hands
pietà in the dell.

Doctor. Preacher. Bible salesman.
Man. There was nothing I could be.

How do you feel?
Afraid
How do you feel?
Cold

If I could have kept you alive
or blessed you
I would have stayed
but I was nothing to your old woman or you.
She knew it of course and kept calling for Jesus.
It was almost one.
She would be gone by two,
and so I left you
no worse off than you were,
your puckered sockets sucking
the balls of your eyes,
your lopsided head to a hand
it could fall to home in.
I looked for the heart behind me
pumping its light
into the hardened arteries of the air.
The only thing there
was kudzu come to take the road again.

3

At first you were something that happened
out of Natchez
do not cross solid line

and then you were something that happens every day.
Damn you friend
and your wife
and your Buick car
(the time is one minute till five on all clocks).
Memory. Magician. Ghost. Whatever you are
I never saved your life,
do not deserve
or want such faithfulness.

I did what I could.

For weeks I turned through papers death by death
by Johnson by Givens by Washington Smith
at home
after an extended illness

survived by me.

Who is to blame
if the casual ambulance found
neither one of us waited?

4
Man. Unholy meat. Unfastened bones.
It was fifteen years ago and I stare still
at every blue suit with a broken face
wearing a hubcap, pulling a bad leg.

I may start tomorrow reading the stones.

From *The Only World There Is*

If Every Person There Is but One

If every person there is but one
should disappear
and then all cats
birds grass
sea horses trees
all rocks and water and toys
and all planets
and the suns go out and the ashes
blow away in the winds
and the winds go
and that person explodes in bright silence
to atoms
and all the atoms dissolve to darkness
but one
which being the center
of weight and all dimension
can never
no matter how fast
move away
from the middle of nothing,
then moving is not moving.
We have been tricked.

The atom you may say
is also nothing
and so put aside the problem
but let us say
with a fump and flash of light
and a splash of water
everything is back
and I walk across the street,
by what argument do I not
when I get there
stand back where I was
in dead center still?

Think of whatever moves as God
or if nothing moves
think how still we stand.

It Is Not That It Came to Nothing, Emiliano

It is not that it came to nothing, Emiliano.
All things do.
It is that it came
in a slow land
so quickly true.

There is a rope
a campesino
will take a tourist to see
for two pesos
that has not even rotted from the tree.

It is not that he died for nothing
Emiliano.
So all men die.
It is that he went
in a slow land
so suddenly by.

There is a temple
a precarious cone of rocks some men built here
before Christ
to please the seasons and divide the year.

It is not that your dreams died.
Dreams do.
All dreams are grass.
It is how soon
Emiliano
it came to pass.

The Associate Professor (Mad Scientist)
to (His Love) His Student
in Physics 100 Lab

What you have to know
F = MA
is what you have to know

a slow truck can break you
quick
as a fast brick

two that want love a little will lay
more likely than one
wanting love a lot

if God is anything more than simply not
He has only barely to be
so capital is the G

and you
if you turn your head
can
as a matter of course
dismiss my class

if you turned your body and
smiled
immorally illegally
[I wonder

[what could I do]
with such a sudden force
with such a mass

GOD = STUDENT

/ LUST

Plain

Out of Mobile I saw a rusty Ford
fingers wrapped like pieces of rope
around the steering wheel
foxtail flapping the head of the hood
of the first thing ever
he has called his own.

Between two Bardahls
above the STP
the flag flies backwards
[Go to Church This Sunday] *
Support Your Local Police
Post 83
They say the same thing
[They say
I am not alone.

Let Me Tell You   *what?*

how to do it from the beginning.
First notice everything:
The stain on the wallpaper
of the vacant house,
the mothball smell
of a Greyhound toilet.
Miss nothing. Memorize it.
You cannot twist the fact you do not know.

Remember
the blonde girl you saw in the bar.
Put a scar on her breast.
Say she left home to get away from her father.
Invent whatever will support your line.
Leave out the rest.

Use metaphors: The mayor is a pig
is a metaphor
which is not to suggest
it is not a fact.
Which is irrelevant.
Nothing is less important
than a fact.

Be suspicious of any word you learned
and were proud of learning.
It will go bad.
It will fall off the page.

When your father lies
in the last light
and your mother cries for him,
listen to the sound of her crying.
When your father dies
take notes
somewhere inside.

If there is a heaven
he will forgive you
if the line you found was a good line.

It does not have to be worth the dying.

28

Today Is Wednesday

which is the day I have decided to understand.
I have tried since morning.
Now for the second time
my shadow is longer than I am
and still I can't understand.

I have asked everyone to help me.
I asked the bus driver to help me.

He said, *My name is John Foster Kelley*
which is a name you will need.

I asked the waitress with mustard
on her mouth.
She said, *I have a surgical*   frailty
scar on my belly.

I asked a policeman. I said,
Today is Wednesday.
He said, *Go ask your mother.*
I asked my mother.

I never saw you before in my life

son.

Tomorrow is Thursday.
Thursday I will understand.
If I can find the right bus
the right café
I will say,
Somebody help me.

Friday I will find myself
the one who can help me.

I will recognize it at once,
breasts of a big woman
face of a dog
the hinder parts held high
as a camel rises
in the unheated intergalactic spaces
under the gray blanket of my
most dry dreams.

I will say, *What about the whales?*

and it will be done.
Friday I will do it myself.

Then I will tell everyone my understanding.
At first, of course, they will not hear,
and when they do they will not allow me near
inhabited places.
I will grow old sending in scribbled notes
tied to the teats of cows and the tails of goats.

Voice of America

Do not imagine his father lying
between his mother and falling to sleep
beside her while she wonders how
she knows, knowing she will keep

the secret for a weaker proof.
Do not imagine the millionth seed
moving by some myotic hunger
from dark to dark, from need to need.

Do not imagine that it by luck
or fate finds the target to win
and like a bullet hitting a head
in slow motion crashes in.

Do not imagine the man starts
and terminates in the same act,
will be before the bullet stops
the zero absolute unfact

his mother remembered in reverse.
Do not imagine his father sent
the million missiles against the egg
with more joy and less intent.

Do not imagine the cells splitting.
Do not imagine the hollow ball
he was awhile, a senseless worm,
no heart, head, nothing at all,

as when his father a following day
the following month would ask, "What is it?"
"It's nothing. It's honestly nothing at all."
Do not imagine the exquisite

danger when the cell divides
when a chromosome splits apart
half shifting here, half there,
to shape the kidney and the heart.

Do not imagine the enormous eyes.
Do not imagine the chin sits
soft against the uncovered heart.
Do not imagine the gill slits,

the hands unfinished, the tail shrinking.
Do not imagine the time at hand
or what it means. Raise the gun.
Hold it gently as you were trained

to hold it. Let the bullet swim
slowly into his opening head
fast as sperm   the way the films
in school can show a flower spread.

31

How the Elephant Got His Hump

for John Christman

Consider a fact: an olive
(unlike cherries and boysen-
berries and beans) begins
as a most potent poison.

An olive grower of course
and biochemist know what'll
make it the bitter and dun
hors d'oeuvre we buy in a bottle.

The olive is soaked in lye
for twenty days and turned
on every one of the twenty
to keep it from being burned

then soaked in the juice of pickles
and turned every day,
which renders the amine soluble
enough to be leached away,

the amine being the problem,
which amine being bound
to a protein makes an olive
which falls upon the ground

so deadly quick a poison,
which is why the lye
has first to break the bond,
which of course is why

no man of the Middle East
or beast has ever been seen—
or seen again if he was—
eating an olive green.

The question before the house:
Since the receipt is now
4,000 years old at least,
who found it out, and how?

Well, I have a fancy.
Imagine the High Priest
Lord Executioner
of all the Middle East

preparing to put to death
a breaker of taboos
who diddled the temple virgins
and never paid his dues

in the shabby lodge he lived in
and pissed in the sacred pool,
slept at sacrifices
and toyed with his tool,

until he roused the anger
of elders and—what was worse—
perverse admiration,
until a public curse

was said upon his head.
The High Priest swore to make
a more than common end,
and set about to take

the fruit which was by custom
exquisite execution,
to cook it first in a caustic,
second an acid, solution.

When he contemplated
the agony in his hand
he could only smile
that he could understand

how he had come to be
the number one High Priest
Lord Executioner
of all the Middle East.

To make more perfect perfection
and imperfect people the humbler
he poured the coup de grace,
two poisons in a tumbler,

juice of the fruit and grain
said to drive men mad,
and mixed them 5 to 1
by chance and knew he had,

when he dropped in the olive,
such agony in the cup
that he could scarcely speak
to summon the buglers up

to the top of the highest hill
where desert turns to sky
to summon the people in
to watch the heretic die.

The heretic, being of gentle
birth albeit a fool,
was set to lose his life
but would not lose his cool.

He took the drink as told to
and killed it in a swallow
and asked his host politely
if there was more to follow.

He nibbled the olive, even,
to take fate's roughest ration,
and spat the pit at the people
and posed in a manly fashion

and was not less surprised
to find he would not die
than those prostrate about him
who called him Highest of High.

As King he showed his people
his powers were still alive
by drinking a draft of poison
each afternoon at five

for all the years of his reign,
which were forty and four,
and said that it was good
and often called for more,

prepared of course by him
who once was Lord High Priest,
who now was Royal Mixer
to the King of the Middle East.

The House in the Vacant Lot

Cutting across a vacant lot,
I felt concrete under my feet
and found myself at the front door
of a house that was not there anymore.

I traced the walls by where the grass
was thin and came again to the spot
where the entrance hall had been.
I let myself as it seemed to me in

and wandered through the disappeared
and long-forgotten rooms. Some glass
and a broken brick were all that was left
of the rooms where people had kissed and slept

alone once and then together.
I thought of this until a weird
or common thought took hold of my head:
Why do I think of the past as dead?

Am I a person present and real
walking through a house that by chance
was and is not or am I he
who am not but who will be,

inverse of common thought

who steps through real and present brick?
Or am I here and the house here still?
Is some woman's heartbeat quicker
when she sees the candle flicker

He already feels alone—

in a closed room? Are we together?
Does such commingling twist and crack
windows I walk through? Does a cold fear
come? Do they wonder if I walk here?

He b/c the ghost —

When a glass tumbles does the mother
cross herself? Does the priest
come to say that I am Christ
or exorcise the poltergeist?

In Your Own Words without Lying
Tell Something of Your Background
with Particular Attention
to Anything Relating to the Position
for Which You Are Applying. Press Down.

Pressing down, I remember
the night my father
and mother will have forgotten.
She filled the lamps in the kitchen
he slung the washing water on the ground
chickens scattered squawking;
the sound of the pump primed
the cold zinc of the dipper
water down the chin
a mumbled word
and the long yawn at last
that leaves the body hollow as a gourd
when the vegetable skin
goes brown and hard   *decay*
under the thick green vines
in the dry yard.

And they went to bed   *His own*
the night I came together   *conception?*
and began.

I may have been describing the night
my grandfather
emptied himself of my father   *His father's*
and my never uncles.   *conception?*

There was no way to tell the difference
in those nights.

I think that was the first important thing.

I was covered when I was five
like Job with boils
they shaved my head
peeled the cloth away from the bed
in the morning.
The neighbors came to call
said, What have you done
that God has put this affliction on your son?
When I was eleven I went to sleep
with a gothic radio underneath the quilt
the glowing grin of the dial
bright as the guilt I manufactured there.

Saturday night the Grand Old Hayride
There's A Great Speckled Bird
Flying Somewhere
But I Didn't Hear Nobody Pray.

Sunday nights I listened to the prophets,
how faith washes sins and Catholics away:

This is Brother Bob's Good Old Gospel Hour
Our time is almost
send your dimes and dollars
The Bible Man
B-I-B-L-E
We depend to help us carry on
to the first two thousand
a plastic tablecloth
that glows
in the dark
with the face of Jesus.

Imagine what your friends and neighbors will say

while the choir sings one more time
in the background softly

and tenderly Jesus is calling,
O Sinner Come Home.

Monday Miss Gardner began the fifth grade
took up the marbles
let Big Butt Butler erase the board
never me
sent sealed messages to other rooms
by Salina Mae who was already starting
to have tits Walter said were got
from doing it.

O.D. showed what he had behind the gin
always after Salina Mae was gone
and Mary Sue let us look if we begged her.

Walter drowned.
O.D. is a doctor. Mary Sue married
a preacher and has children.
Salina Mae I will tell you about.

One Saturday afternoon we made believe.

That is all I can tell.

On my grandfather's farm
there was a river we swam in
there was an old bell to call us back.

Love Poem

Six o'clock
and the sun rises across the river.
The traffic cop wakes up
and crawls over his wife.
The naked professor will sleep another hour.
The dentist wakes up and reaches for a smoke.
The doctor reaches for the phone
and prescribes,
his voice full of rust.
The shoe clerk wakes to his clock,
touches himself,
and lies listening to his woman in the shower.

It is midnight now in Samoa.

Nine o'clock
and the school bell rings.
Miss Gardner taps her ruler on the desk.
She calls the roll.
Oscar Carpenter is absent.
He does not like the sound of the ruler.

It is midnight now in Osaka.

Eleven o'clock:
The salesman makes his way past dogs and wheels,
his knuckles already sore,
hoping for bells.

On Maple Street the policeman's wife
shuts her kimono slowly and shuts the door.
On Willow Street the professor's wife
tells him about her cousin in Mineral Wells
who was also a salesman but never amounted to much.

On Juniper Street the dentist's wife
is drunk and lets him have her on the floor,
says she will get a divorce.
Says she will see him again, of course, if she can.

It is midnight now in Djakarta.

Five o'clock
and the men are coming home.
The traffic cop comes home,
his ears in his pockets.
The doctor comes home,
the sun slipping down his forehead.
The shoe clerk comes,
the uncertain knees
still fitting the sockets of his eyes.

It is midnight now in Berlin.

Six o'clock:
The streetlights come on.

It is midnight now in Bordeaux.

Ten o'clock:
In Mercy Hospital a man is dying.
His brain
squeezes all his thoughts to one thought,
squeezes that to nothing
and lets go.

It is midnight now in La Paz.

Eleven o'clock:
The children are gone to bed and we are here
sitting across the room from one another,
accustomed to this house
that is not ours to keep,
to this world that is not ours,
and to each other.

Sands run through the children in their sleep.

ANTI-WHITMAN

micro- macro-

erasure

Lost letter

La Ultima Carta: A Young Wife Writes to Her Husband in the Mountains

I make a Y
brittle as dry wood.
The sputtering pen splits open
unwrites words I could not have mailed.

Saturday I sat by the lake,
pretended to read letters
that have not come.
They are too brief and tell me you are well.
(I am not sure I believe them.)

WORLD'S UNCOOPERATIVES

CHILE

> doubt

Under my hand, Husband,
brooms break
corn grinds to sand.

You have no faith in spirits
would claim the water
dripping from a tap at night
means nothing
that a wind coming down to the coast
out of those hills is neither alive nor dead
but I listen for signs

and forgive me this:
when the wind
brushes against the curtain
touches my sheet
I tense to feel the fingers of a ghost.

I look through my eyes in the morning mirror
afraid I will conjure you
trying to conjure you there
but all I see are the days spinning back
with the strange quiet violence of dreams.

Sra. Cortinez whose son was a good soldier
is also alone and knows she is going
to be alone. I envy her knowing
for certain. Forgive me.

I sit up late
after unweaving myself
and write you letters
and every time the thought comes
that you may go and I not
know about it,

that I may write a month
after your death
to tell you things
as one talks meaningfully with gestures
to a friend who half a block back
has stopped at some store,
that I will hold your picture
focus on your mouth
to remember you more
while in some obscene place
a snake is crawling through your face.

I tell you my unfaithfulness
my unforgivable sin
that I am no longer sure my letters
keep you alive

but I will keep on writing
until we win
what we are fighting for
whoever we are.

From *Halfway from Hoxie*

Villanelle – 19 lines – divided into 5 tercets + a quatrain

alternating refrain

long time in Chile

Highly formal — dance

dancing & poetry writing

For Jordan with Love
the Eighth Year of the Slaughter:
A Minuet for Army Boots and Orchestra

Ref.

act

reality psyche

Whose tongues are twisted and whose hearts are shrunk
may (play) as puppets, may in that disguise *forget*
while villages burn in their brains, (drink to be drunk.)

Apocalypse

So when God comes to catch this crumbling chunk
of dirt, what do we say? That we (despise)
whose tongues are twisted and whose hearts are shrunk?

No sympathy?

doubting disciple – what diff.?

If Thomas had told us the gnawed body stunk,
what would it change? Men knowing what men devise
while villages burn in their brains, (drink to be drunk)

Is this a to be or not to world?

If Calvin came to tell us Christ is bunk, *Deep Skepticism*
what could he hope to teach us? Pain? Surprise?
Whose tongues are twisted and whose hearts are shrunk?

So the Viking sails for home and is sunk,
so Napoleon is poisoned, so Lorca dies,
while villages burn in their brains. Drink to be drunk

wife – as if they are abducted

QUATRAIN

until they lay (us) to sleep and slam the trunk,
two people more who open and close their eyes, *blink*
whose tongues are twisted and whose hearts are shrunk,
while villages burn in their brains. Drink to be drunk.

Love poem?

44

Remembering Walter

I remember when I learned he was dead.
I was halfway done with a paper route
and saw the crowd and stopped to find out
what was going on and someone said

Walter was drowned. I had to go disguised
in a borrowed Boy Scout uniform to take
my turn sitting beside him at the wake,
to halfway hope the skin across his eyes

would tighten against the light. I would find mud
to bless them open or find whoever knew
what it was you had to say or do.
But someone said he didn't have his blood. | *embalmed*

What should these memories mean at forty-two?
That twelve is a highly impressionable age. *Poet*
That all the rage we learn is the first rage.
That more than choose to die by water, do. ⟩ *wasteland allusion*

The Neighbor

No one knows what the banging is all about
or the drilling that buzzes like a swarm of gnats
above the clover between his woods and the wash

or why it is he never came into the store
to pick up his almanac
or goes to Grange anymore

or why his sons have all come back from the city
and their fair wives with them

or why he walks the long fences of his farm
picking up sometimes a twig
turning it in his fingers
and letting it fall.

The main fact is, which does make us uneasy,
he's set about building something in his barn

and it's big.

IRONY?

Thinking Friday Night
with a Gothic Storm Going
about Final Causes and Logos
and Mitzi Mayfair

Was the Word and the Word was just
a swelling in the ether. Dust

that would seem wind, sun, earth, and sea
had not come to seem to be

and ether was only force compacted.
So are we. Though we have acted

like stuff, we know that we are not.
We are spume and a sunspot.

This man that seems to know its name
is a waterspout, a flame,

a whirlpool, a funnel storm
where nothing stays except the form

the funnel is. We are nothing
but energy in love, come huffing

and puffing our way through what we take
as time and space, as wine and steak.

This is philosophy I think
and science and a waste of ink.

And still I know the shape I touch
that seems something is nothing much,

is only a moving, and we are dreams
we have about us. The earth that seems

rocks and water is only force
moving through a shape. The source,

they will say, of rhyme and the seasons
but we have our own good reasons

for holding to the old confusions
of form and thing. What but illusions

matter at all when all things
are what they do? A wasp's wings,

for instance, and you, as I am a node
energy moves through, coming as food

drink, salt, sunlight, air,
and leaving as heat, spit, hair,

tears, toenails, words, and sperm.
Lord bless the lowly worm

who is also form in flux
and does not know or care and fucks

such as he does without the stinking
thoughts we always come to thinking.

Darling, let us learn to move
like that again—apparent you

force and form, vis-à-vis
form and force, apparent me—

riding the storm all words are about
till the storm stops, played out.

✛ Vision and Prayer

Christ that as the maggot
Takes unto himself our putrefaction
Cleanse us now and in the hour of our death

Christ that as the maggot
Comes not for the clean
Cleanse us now and in the hour of our death

Christ that as the maggot
Comes from the grave and grows wings
Cleanse us now and in the hour of our death

Christ that as the maggot
Is with us always
Cleanse us now and in the hour of our death

Maggot of God that eats away
The corruption of the world
Cleanse Bless us now and in the hour of our death

Sitting Alone at Sunrise:
Problems in the Space-Time Continuum

If in the future
a time traveler
comes back to this moment
he's here now.

At 15,000 feet you see a car
run off a country road and turn over.
It's already a county away.
Take the coffee.

There will come a year
when one by one your friends
thumbing past your last address
will think to mark through it.

If I could be
in two places at once
I would be with you twice
all the time.

I Go Out of the House for the First Time

I go out of the house for the first time
since the day everybody found out
and the first person I meet says hello turd
so I pull off my ears I have always had
distinctive ears and drop them in a trash
dispenser in front of The Farmers Bank and a man
coming out of the bank says hello turd
so I twist off my nose as people have always
noticed my nose in particular and drop it in
the book deposit in front of the city library
and a woman coming out of the library says
hello turd and I begin to see
how difficult disguises are and pluck
my left eye out as people have always noticed
my eyes are most particularly well matched
and swallow it down as there is no place to put it
and a small boy up a lamp pole says
hello turd so I take off my clothes
as people have always commented on my clothes
and I walk down the street and a little girl
playing jacks on the sidewalk sees me and says
hello turd so I pull off my penis
and everybody runs up saying in loud voices
look at the dumb turd he pulled off his penis.

On the Symbolic Consideration of Hands
and the Significance of Death

Watch people stop by bodies in funeral homes.
You know their eyes will fix on the hands and they do.
Because a hand that has no desire to make
a fist again or cut bread or lay stones
is among those things most difficult to believe.
It is believed for a fact by a very few
old nuns in France who carve beads out of knuckle bones.

And Then

Your toothbrush won't remember your mouth
Your shoes won't remember your feet

Your wife one good morning
will remember your weight
will feel unfaithful
throwing the toothbrush away
dropping the shoes in the Salvation Army box
will set your picture in the living room

Someone wearing a coat you would not have worn
will ask was that your husband
she will say yes

A Toast to Floyd Collins

To Mitzi Mayfair
To Jesus Christ Man of a Thousand Faces
To Lev Davidovich Trotsky
To Nicanor Parra

To whoever dies tonight in New Orleans
To Operator 7 in Kansas City

To the sound of a car crossing a wooden bridge
To the Unified Field Theory
To the Key of F

And while I'm at it
A toast to Jim Beam
To all the ice cubes thereunto appertaining
To Jordan knitting
A silver cat asleep in her lap
And the sun going down

Which is the explanation for everything

Think of Judas That He Did Love Jesus
for Walter Weiss

I

Think of Judas that he did love Jesus,
that he for simple grace came and for glory
out of a thinness of days to a mad band.
That he was filled of his fathers and full with fury.
That it came to him to force the Master's hand.
That it came to him to have the battle begun.
That it came to him that when the Lord will have won
he would see the Son of Man a King
who being gentle would not have had it done
for all the helmets split and the blood spilled.

Think that when he sees how Christ is killed
he does the only thing he knows to do,
goes not with God but goes another way
from the plain man he never meant to betray.

II

Or think of Judas filled with sin and fears
afraid to tell his name, or name the burning
torments turning like scorpions over his skin.

Think that Jesus who needs to be betrayed
chooses anxious Judas for his friend
and uses Judas to God's and the devil's end.

Think how Judas knows that Jesus knew,
knowing all hearts, what Judas would come to do.
Think that Judas recognizes the role
played half in shadow with a short line to speak,
knows he is poor of spirit and sufficiently weak
for which and no plain love he was called to this.
And curses Christ who knowing he was faithful
to both their purposes cast him for such a kiss.

And curses himself who curses first the Lord
who alone is the Lord and leads himself away
with a bought rope from trust he did not betray.

III

Or think of Judas. As anyone can tell
Judas is bad. Jesus is good and betrayed
for cash and badness. Judas is afraid
and finds a tree and hangs himself upon it
and holds his fist that none of the fee fall
to the watchful beggars. His name is lust for money,
disgrace before God and men and broken trust.
Is shame. Is everlasting as the unspoken name.

IV

These are the stories of Judas that fill the spaces
inside the story of Judas. Look quickly
behind the words you have heard and uncover creatures
looking the other way with words in their hands,
words of the unseen heart of Herod and of Caesar
and even of us. Or is it better
to listen to the preachers, what they say,
believing in the gospel but not in the ghosts
haunting our histories, our papers, our simplest books,
turning invisibly toward us at every word
with round, incredulous, and desperate looks.

From *Why God Permits Evil*

Where to Turn When Sorrow Comes
like a Black Bull in Your Dreams

Start with the house: the smell of the person dead,
heavy and vaguely accusing and then gone;
bedpillow, shoes, and hat, and preferred chair,
like half-domesticated animals
finding their first ways.

Start with the death:
friends coming with ancient platters; the altered kin
entering rooms as quietly as spies,
whispering comfort like a dangerous secret;
the journey behind the hearse, with every word
irrelevant and thin) and all the faces
around the grave turned off and folded down.
Then home again, where as if a train
began to move, the closed and numbered days
bump past going gradually faster.

Start with the signs:
Pain in the chest. Headaches. Bad dreams.
The reaming finger with its little condom;
the apologetic needle; the sphygmomanometer,
its one egg panting in the doctor's palm;
the X ray's nostrils sniffing into places
invisibly scarlet. Each one having the right,
they wait behind their warrants with long words
for any person whose name is inscribed there
to sit or stand up or stop to count change
or stop the car in line at a traffic light
or lean forward to reach for the radio.

Begin with beginnings: a man and a woman lie down.
It all becomes right, abstract, and natural.

But death is a robber. Death is a son of a bitch.

Go back to the grave then and stand
crying like a child.

Everyone Dies in a Light Rain

lying on the highway
surrounded by strangers

This is what the *Oxford English
Dictionary* tells us
the *Atlanta Constitution* tells us
and the *World Almanac*
and the girl at the counter
in the Frank and Louise Café

This is what
the telephone number
in the toilet stall
tells us
The rodeo rider
holding the rope in one hand
the horse an arc beneath him
the other hand floating
tells us again
The white telephone
by the white bed
in the round room
tells us again

as also the inverted car
tells us
cars and pickup trucks pulling off and idling
on the slick shoulder
anybody hurt
and then someone waving the traffic on
the arm repeating its small important circle
as proud as anarchy
ordained as law
as we edge obediently by the cold radiant place

and drive awhile without saying anything
as if we were turning something
over in our minds

Potter, Vidalia

Vidalia Potter (who often as not
put sheet to show and quilt underneath
when she made the bed and always forgot

the social worker woman's name
and made coffee that went to waste
every time the woman came,

who fretted about a festering sore
on one of the legs of one of the girls
and walked at six to the Safeway store

for bottle drinks—Dr. Pepper,
Strawberry Creme, a 7Up—
bread and sliced bologna for supper,

who never was sick and never was well,
whose man had a job at the chicken plant
and told time by the quitting bell,

who loved her children as best she could
and washed the leg and swept the floor
sometimes and thought about the good

strong-smelling man who called her to bed
when he wasn't drunk and he wasn't tired)
never could get it fixed in her head
what the social worker said.

WWI

Still we turn a corner and there it is—
the trenches, the green gas,
the helmets like hubcaps,
the bombs small enough for a man
to die alone in,
the mademoiselle from Armentières, the mud,
those square little planes like canvas box kites.
What is it we keep trying to remember?
Wilfred Owen died. That wasn't it.
Long lines who never heard of Wilfred Owen
synchronize their watches and crawl under barbed wire
looking for something,
maybe a map,
a canteen with brandy still in it.
And what would brandy taste like
after all that time.
Good. It tastes good.

The Unknown Sailor

sits up in bed in his navy robe
and looks at the wall or whatever moves
between his bed and the wall and neither
approves nor disapproves.

No one knows his name or his town
or even his country. In forty-four
a hospital ship in Boston harbor
put him ashore

with the label Navy and nothing else.
For those thin years he has never spoken.
He smiles and blinks in a white silence
occasionally broken

by wives and sons and daughters and friends
of men who went to war and were lost
and never found. They leave with another
sailor crossed—

or soldier, merchant marine, or marine—
from a nameless list. Be grateful for that.
Here in the ward he may have an inkling
of where he's at.

Those lives he moved among before
have long since filled the space and the town
has closed the way the sea closes
when ships go down.

Prison

Past Mobile Home Estates,
past the Pentecostal Campgrounds,
past a barn,
its roof lying beside it,   *decay*
a shack of unpainted planks
in a soybean field,
an empty houseboat rotting in a green river.

A crop-dusting biplane set down by the highway ahead
turns itself into an irrigation pump
when the car gets close.

You turn off 65 on the prison road.
There are hundreds of reasons for being on 65
but not for being on the prison road.
You feel somebody shifting inside of you
pushing your parts around. You believe it now.
This is where it starts. ↑ *prison*

Whites for the short hairs. They don't fit.
Tough shit. Go tell the boss
you quit.
What you do is fit the clothes.
Hands at your sides in single rows.
Don't touch the wall
unless you want to wash the hall
with your tongue and your piss and a bar of soap.
You will behave and be well. We hope.
You will bear in mind, if we rankle you some,
nobody here asked you to come.

What is there to say?
There may
be some small difference in one day
and the next and the next but there's no way
to name the difference, like a lay
in some whorehouse wherein they
all have the same look when you pay
only they never mean you to stay.
Except for this, what's there to say?

Some days there is a settling into the tomb.
Some nights there come whole years a man forgets
his wife and children and his unpaid debts
and prays for wet dreams and a bad sense of time.

Dear friend: She runs around. A friend.

Lord I want to go home, which is a small town
where I live with a lady who surely goes out   YEHH
but would not let another man lie down   RIGHT
between the long legs that I dream about.

You stay yourself in a world of your mind's making. |
Bones is the only man ever sent to jail
for buggery with a banty rooster. They tell
how they brought him to court with the swollen chicken
still stuck on, flapping its wings and squawking.

Ten years and mercy and a thin smile
before the board and after a little while
the gate opens and you feel your guts
pull tight and you go out and the gate shuts
and what you feel then is sharply the same
as that white fear you felt the day you came.
There will be a job. And a woman. And a telephone.
But first you will rent a room. And be drunk. And alone.

But flat time friend is ten years.
But even that friend disappears
day by day though days grow long
when nights are short and walls are strong
and food is flat and beds are hard
and there's a meanness in every guard
and the family coming to bring you cheer
grows a little stranger year by year.

For Fred Carpenter Who Died in His Sleep

Penniless to our surprise
at the peak of his earning power he lies:
a man of the mean, who rarely meant
much harm, and nearly always spent
his money well; who got his views
from *Newsweek* and *U.S. News*
(though he trusted only the latter)
and wondered often what was the matter
with those there was something the matter with
(some being his kin and kith)
and believed what was right or discreetly done
was right, and looked for a little fun
when he traveled out of town
and wished his woman would go down
but she never would. He understood.

Footnote on the Invention of Small Pleasures

Young Adam surely must
being newly from dust
the only human life
and with no word for wife
have been somewhat perplexed
to find himself so sexed.

It's Hard to Think the Brain

a ball of ropey dough
should have invented pain
or come to know

how there are things we lend
a fragile credence to
and hope to comprehend
but never do.

And Then I Headed on Back Home

I went to New York and went to the poet's address,
four flights up in a building with clean windows.
He asked what I wanted. He didn't open the door.
I told him I liked his poems and came to say so.
He said if that's true I thank you very much.
I told him his milk was out there getting warm.

Everything Is Fine Here. How Are You?

She blinks above her sunglasses at the man
putting the letters up on the movie marquee.
Along the wire he slides an S, an N.
His sleeves are cut away. The marguerita
she presses against her mouth. She feels her mouth
suck in against the salt. She watches the man
test his way descending the stepladder
and jerk it spraddled across the sidewalk.
The sound has her in front of a shingled house,
her mother pushing the screen door open, calling
always. She watches him climb the ladder again.
If she passes that way and speaks to him
he will go off and leave her in a grove of oaks,
the twisted bra knotted about her wrists,
the panties stuffed in her mouth, the eyes,
her own eyes, paying no attention.

Reading the Newspaper on Microfilm

I let it go for the fact of it fast as it will,
pages and days sliding by in a gray blur,
black spaces falling before the headlines
marking the nights and mornings until I can tell
Sundays by their length and the running colors,
department store ads from news from real estate
by normal sequence and shifting densities.
I almost wonder, if I watched it long enough,
could I tell the car wrecks from the weddings,
weddings from rapes and fires and book reviews.
The names in accidents and baseball scores
for months pass by in minutes. I see
that I have stayed from April into autumn
and think of a mind that saw it all go by
as fast as that in the first place and wonder at it.

On Hearing about the Death of Mitzi Mayfair

Hurrah for the next
man that dies
said Errol Flynn
and someone
snuck open the earth
and let him in.

Jesus died legend has it on dogwood
whose blossom for that reason
cursed itself into a cross.
The small red spot
at the tip of each plain petal
spread just at the Easter season
we say is the blood but it isn't.
You know it's not.

I close my eyes and see a calendar
with a date circled in red.

The trouble is that
my madness
was not the other half
of your madness.

There has never been a poem
to explain anything.
For that reason
many people who would otherwise
write poems do not.
Praise such people.

On the Way Home from Nowhere, New Year's Eve

For papers I think I need, we bump off
the street and stop. I leave the engine on,
mean to make my way to the buzzing light
above the back door, but the door is dark.
Old Main's a hulking, dull, uncertain form,
no windows and no size. Then I remember

one small truth I didn't mean to remember,
that all the lights at ten would be turned off
for somebody's purpose. I enter the hollow form,
try one time to flick the light switch on
and shrug my way into the seamless dark.
What outside seemed scattered, useless light

would be a brilliance here. Reflections. Moonlight.
Sensing my way between the walls I remember
old mythologies of daytime and the dark
spun by gods and monster movies, cast off
with ignorance. My fingers stumble on
another switch. Nothing. I feel my form

SESTINA.
6 - 6 lines
6 STANZAS
envoi

7 FORM
7 Remember

STUMBLING
FORM IN
BUILDING

64

falling away into another form.
I hear the hound, look for the quick light
glancing out of his eyes and imagine my own
open, aimless, milky. I remember
what children think of when the lights are off.
Something brushing the hand. To fit the dark

I tell myself I am blind. In such a dark
I could be moving down the spaceless form
of time, a painted tunnel. I twist off
my shoes and walk in deafness. Leap. Grow light
for one slow moment, then loose parts remember
gravity. I twist the sounds back on.

I'm over a million years old and going on
thirteen. I've always been afraid of the dark.
There truly are warlocks, witches, and I remember
banshees, saints and the always shifting form
of Satan himself. I feel a fly light
and crawl across my forehead. I brush it off.

Going on, I grab some papers off
some desk in the dark and turn back toward the light
I barely remember, running, hungry for form.

Picker

Uvalde Texas to Nashville Tennessee
is near as a tavern jukebox, is twice as far
as Jesus to Judas, as a rusty Plymouth car
to a bus with a bedroom. We look outside to see

hundreds come honking to listen to whistle to praise
the picker among us, come to tell us again
about the differences, as mostly between
how we imagine marriage those quick days

till we do marry, and how we learn to live
together after with the debts and beer
and strangers' crotches open everywhere.
I watch to learn the life you learn to give

to tell the love and sickness in our skin
and neon lights and darkness. Lord we crave
those words for hardness of our bones, to save
the soul from puffiness. You put us in

flat touch with what we are, and make that touch
bearable first, then almost pleasant and then
plain necessary, how we try to mend
our nervous ways for nothing and drink too much

and want bad love. I listen to you sing
while lean red faces eat you up alive
to know by what bright secrets we survive
the flesh's soft transgressions. No rhyming thing

will give the sense men want of who they are.
Or undo the differences we didn't mean
to deal with once—as for instance between
the bus with the bedroom and the rusty car.

Which is a green distance and does grow
while the car in the side mirror shrinks away
and you want to touch the driver's shoulder and say,
Man, we're going too fast. You don't though.

Memphis, 2:00 P.M.

I saw a woman getting out of a car.
She said to the man in the car
leave me alone.
She closed the door with both hands.
She said to the man please
just leave me alone.

It was a new Plymouth,
blue with a white top.

Husband

She's late. He mixes another drink.
He turns on the television and watches
a woman kissing the wrong man.
He looks at his watch. He feels close
to the cat. Well Cat, he says.
He feels foolish.
He mixes another drink and stands
turning the stem of the glass
back and forth in his fingers.

This also makes him feel foolish.
He looks at his watch. Well Cat, he says.
Lights turn into the driveway.
He slumps into his chair. He
kicks off his shoes and spreads
the open newspaper peacefully
over his face.
He hears the tiny grating of the key.
His heart knocks to get out.

monostich

After You Die You Don't Give a Piddling Damn

I do, Lord, I do. Therefore I am.

How to Stop Smoking

If you are a man
think of a woman wiggling out of her underwear
saying come on you don't have to love me.

If you are a woman
think of the man thinking that.

Practice.

Why God Permits Evil:
For Answer to This Question
of Interest to Many
Write Bible Answers, Dept. E-7
—ad on a matchbook cover

Of interest to John Calvin and Thomas Aquinas
for instance and Job for instance who never got

one straight answer but only his cattle back.
With interest, which is something, but certainly not

any kind of answer unless you ask
God if God can demonstrate God's power

and God's glory, which is not a question.
You should all be living at this hour.

You had Servetus to burn, the elect to count,
bad eyes and the Institutes to write;

68

you had the exercises and had Latin, *A QViNAS*
the hard bunk and the solitary night;

you had the neighbors to listen to and your woman
yelling at you to curse God and die.   *JoB*

Some of this to be on the right side;
some of it to ask in passing, Why?

Social satire

Why badness makes its way in a world He made?
How come he looked for twelve and got eleven? *DiSciples*

You had the faith and looked for love, stood pain,
learned patience and little else. We have E-7.

Churches may be shut down everywhere,   *iRonic*
half-written philosophy books be tossed away. *SARCASTICALLY*

Some place on the South Side of Chicago
a lady with wrinkled hose and a small gray

bun of hair sits straight with her knees together
behind a teacher's desk on the third floor

of an old shirt factory, (bankrupt and abandoned)
except for this just cause, and on the door:

Dept. E-7. She opens the letters
asking why God permits it and sends a brown

plain envelope to each return address.
But she is not alone. All up and down

the thin and creaking corridors are doors
and desks behind them: E-6, E-5, 4, 3.

A desk for every question, for how we rise
(blown up and burned) for how the will is free,

for when is Armageddon, for whether dogs
have souls or not and on and on. On

beyond the alphabet and possible numbers
where cross-legged, naked, and alone,

there sits a pale, tall, and long-haired woman
upon a cushion of fleece and eiderdown

holding in one hand a handwritten answer,
holding in the other hand a brown

plain envelope. On either side, cobwebbed
and empty baskets sitting on the floor

say *In* and *Out*. There is no sound in the room.
There is no knob on the door. Or there is no door.

The Friend

I hadn't seen him in twelve years.
He could put his hands between the wall
and a light and make a roller coaster
a kidney machine a split T
running a double reverse.
I heard he was in town so of course I invited him.
I took down a picture to have a blank space
on the wall.
Everyone gathered in a semicircle.
I turned off all the lights except one lamp.
Go ahead, I said.
He made a dog.
Then he made a rabbit. It only had one ear.
The elephant didn't have a trunk
and looked like a cow.
Jesus Christ, I said, What happened.
I could hear someone across the room
mixing a drink in the dark.

Getting Experience

The first real job I had was delivering drugs
for Jarman's Pharmacy in Bascum, Arkansas.

If everyone was busy or in the back I sold things.
A cloudy woman with pentecostal hair

softly asked for sanitary napkins.
She brought the Kleenex back unwrapped in twenty minutes.

Shame, said Mr. Jarman, we shouldn't make a joke
of that and made me say I'm sorry and fired me.

When I found out what the woman wanted
I had to say I did what everyone said I did.

That or let them know I hadn't heard of Kotex. *cliché*
⌈Better be thought bad than known for stupid.⌋

The first hard fight I had was after school
with Taylor Wardlow West in Bascum, Arkansas.

Ward West chased me home from school when I was lucky.
My father said Ward West was insecure.

Go smile at him, he said, and let him know
you mean to be his friend. My father believed in (love.)

All day I smiled and twisted in my seat to see him
all hate and slump by himself in the back of the room.

After school he sat on my chest and hit me
and then his little brother sat on my chest and hit me.

And then his little sister sat on my chest and hit me.
She made me so ashamed I tried to kick her

and kicked Ward West in the face. When he could see
I was rounding the corner for home. Jesus, Jesus, Jesus.

Next day everybody told me over and over
how I had balls to make those stupid faces,

him the son of a bitch of the whole school,
and how I surely did kick the piss out of him.

Ward had to go to the dentist. Also his father beat him.
He didn't come to school for two days.

Then he left me alone. He said I was crazy.
Everybody thought I was a little crazy.

Although with balls. I just let them say I was.
Better be thought mad than known for stupid.

Choose if you have a choice, head or heart.
They'll never think you're good and sane and smart.

Being Here

The ring of a doorbell
at three in the morning
even before you know who's standing out there
changes not only the face that flies into your head
but shoes also and the backs of chairs and the repetitions
of wallpaper.
You may say a quick prayer
but anyway you will take it as you have to.

Notes from the Agent on Earth:
[How to Be Human]

In St. Peter's Basilica in the City of Rome
there sits a Holy Father fashioned in marble
encircled by faces well proportioned and doubtless.
His name is Gregory; he spoke for God.
He sits upon a slab; under that slab
the devil, winged and dog-faced, cat-pawed and crooked,
turns in his agony and bares his teeth,
bares his broken claws, turns his nostrils
almost inside out. The statue is his.
One purchases with popes and attendant angels
the privilege of discovering such a devil.
No one could dare to show him by himself.
This loser, this bad and living dream, this Lucifer
alone is more than all the hovering others,
because he carries folded into his face
what no face erased in heaven carries,   *He was banished*
[the fear and loneliness to make us human.]   *Love / Justice are products*
All there is to understand is there.
None here has anything to share with angels.
What makes a human human (more than speech,
a pair of opposable thumbs or the set of the head)
is a cold hand that reaches from under the bed   *Parallel to "One blood sir"*
and closes on your ankle; is lying awake
flat on your back in bed and, becoming aware
your hands are coffin-crossed upon your chest,
not having the little courage to leave them there.
And the girl in the hotel lobby, lost in her fat,
forgetting the room of the man who likes her like that.
[The woman with buttons on her back undone]
to show she doesn't live with anyone.
Think of men and women in nursing homes.   *↑FRAILTY is EQUALIZER*
These were senators, some of them, and bankers,
presidents of colleges, detectives,
people who passed laws, wrote books,
gave loans, found clues, presided over professors,
crying all night in thin metal beds for their mothers,
calling in high voices daddy daddy,   *Communion*
and mother and daddy dead for thirty years.

*What we have in common and what we know
from Loneliness and Fear, called Adam and Eve,
and all we have to turn our hands to
are Love, Ambition, Faith, the Sense of Death.

Love is Fear and Loneliness fed and sleeping;
Faith is Fear and Loneliness explained,
denied and dealt in; Ambition which is envy
is Fear and Loneliness coming up to get you;
Death is Fear and Loneliness fading out.
This is the stuff of life and the gospel of art.
So art and life are much alike in this,
though art, because we see both ends, can please us.
We never know if life is a cave or a tunnel.
We only know we spend the days going deeper,
feeling around for the nature of good and evil,
although the only question with an answer that matters
is whether we have a little free will or none.

But this is only content; this is stuffing.
Flesh is distastefully still and marble is rock
without the patterns a body pushes through.
So life and art are much alike in this.
Life is change that finds a changing pattern;
art is change we put a pattern to.
And so is sport and war and merchandising.
There is a difference but it doesn't matter.

The old nun who believes in nothing
crosses herself sitting down to supper
and men and women living in New Orleans
dress in the brown and orange clothes of autumn
one certain heavy, indistinguishable day.
They call this The First Day of Autumn.
Some women in Messina whose times of mourning
come close together and touch and overlap
wear black into black the last ten years of their lives.

74

This is about Love and how to tell it.
Charles Hammond Walker of South Carolina,
son of Charles and Sue born Sue Ella Hammond,
daughter of Colonel John and Martha Hammond
of Tennessee, got off a plane in Chicago
and got a taxi and got a hotel room,
got a convention badge and a daily paper
and went to a movie house that shows movies
of naked people doing reciprocal things,
remembered when he got inside the movie
to put the plastic badge that had the name
Charles Hammond Walker in his pocket,
sat down and spread the paper across his lap,
took his penis and pulled it out of his pants
into the cool air. Charles Hammond Walker
has a wife who sometimes in South Carolina
goes dreaming up a chance, a quick chance.

There are many stories of contented lovers.
Some people believe them; be careful of these.

One says: I love you and you alone. One says:
I have something to tell you. Please sit down.

This is about Faith and how to tell it.
Think if you saw a ghost you knew was a ghost.
All the questions answered by that knowledge
are questions of Faith, though this defeats the question.
Faith justified by fact is no faith.

Newspapers, no matter how final the news is,
invite subscriptions, which—though business—
is an act of faith in delay, in possibly not.

One says: The Lord is with us. One says:
There is a fountain filled with blood. Amen.

This is about the Will to Power, Envy,
Covetousness, Ambition, maker of popes,
wars, weddings, poems, and county fairs.

A private holding a microphone like a scepter
can bring commanding generals to silence.

Or start with the swollen moment, the blimp saying yes,
the drum major pumping like a piston,
the majorettes spinning their silver spokes,
pulling the band behind them, dividing the crowd;
cables connecting vans to high windows,
cameras scanning the street. Look at the man
putting money into the parking meter.
Watch how the meter runs down, watch how the band
puts down its instruments and disappears,
how the vans pull away, look how the people leave,
the last ones on the last bus standing silent.

One says: He slipped away in the night. One says:
Everybody move up to the next desk.
promotion

This is about Death and how to tell it.

When a man looks down at the back of his hand
and sees the hand of his father he knows he is dying.   ✓

The eyes of people in the last minutes are bright. *Dick.*

One says: Listen. It gets sweet close to the end.
Still it is very important not to be dead,
but the Lord giveth and the Lord taketh away.

✗ Not much that is said of the dead can be believed. ✗

Why God Permits Evil

This is also something about Ambition.
Also Love. And Faith also. And Death.

76

A man who had too much to calculate
had a vision of hell, was afraid of the dark,
knew that he had walked in evil ways,
corrected his wife to death and darkened his children;
had done things besides unspeakably bad
and could not honestly ask for God's forgiveness
as he was only afraid and could never say,
I'm sorry, Lord. He wanted such redemption
as wipes a life not clean but wipes it away.
And thought that he could have it. He spent his means
for fifteen years of the best brains to be had
in mathematics, space-time, and madness
and had him when he was eighty by god
a simple time-machine, which ought not now
bend any imagination out of shape;
went back seventy years to the same town
and found himself at ten delivering papers;
stole the one car there was and ran himself down;
left himself across a wooden sidewalk,
who barely lied to his mother or masturbated
and went directly to heaven if any can.
He could not be the man who killed the boy
because he never lived to be the man,
having died at ten delivering papers,
survived by his parents, grieved by the fifth grade,
the first death by car in the whole county,
killed by a runaway Ford with no driver
or if a driver, none to be found.

There is much that matters. What matters most is survival.
What matters most in survival is learning the names
of things and the names of visions. If the horizon
for an example were real someone could go there
and call back to the rest of us and say,
Here I am standing on the horizon.
But he would see that his friends were standing on it.

No sense of space or time is dependable here.
The difference in time is that we glance back
at those who stayed in time and didn't come with us,
and see ourselves still back there talking to them.
These are illusions, or seem to be illusions.
Leave them alone. What matters most is survival.

Be careful of too much imagination.
This attracts attention. Attention is trouble.
You have to develop competence, of course.
You have to think of doors opening toward you.
Take any pleasure in it and sooner or later
someone will notice your eyes have an absent look.
Someone with a glass in her hand will stop talking
and wait for you to answer. Practice caution.
Tell stories at parties the way you hear them.

Be careful of how the night moves into morning.
When things have gone right the day opens and closes,
one calendar square checked off and done with.
When something is wrong, when you've drunk too much
or had a fight over love or lost money,
the night runs into the morning in sick streaks
like the fluids of a dog run over in the last block.

Be careful of uniforms of any color,
of glass doors with initials painted on them,
of people always willing to go last.
Be careful of workers who have their own desks.
Be very careful of people whose young are hungry
and have large faces, of days set aside
for the celebration of national independence,
of those who are neither lonely nor afraid.

Be careful everywhere. This is a world—
what?—divided. Not as they say divided.
Think of this: running around the planet,
along the equator exactly, an iron fence;
half the population of the planet
stands on either side and shakes the bars
screaming to be let out, to be let in.

From *Distractions*

The True Story of What Happened

Looking out the window, across the room,
I saw a plane heading toward the west.
I thought as I often do when I see a plane
of who might be on board and what they wish
they'd said before they left or not said
to those they love and those they meant to love.
The plane seemed so small at such a distance,
and seemed to move so slowly, it might have been
some little creature crawling across the screen.
It stopped as if to consider that a while,
changed directions slightly and crawled on.   *solitude*

Inside my head two hundred seventy people
including a crew of eleven disappeared
leaving no trace but only vacancies
at typewriters, bedtime, and breakfast. It came so fast
nobody had a hint of what was coming
except for one especially perceptive
flight attendant who seemed to be startled
about something just at the last moment.

Believing

There is a myth
persisting among a few African tribes
and some inhabitants of the Greek Islands
that says a building will not last a year
unless the builder seals inside its walls
the head or heart or body
(depending on the land you hear it in)
of somebody dear,
wife or child or friend
close enough for a sense of sacrifice.

Where could he be I've called and called
Have you seen him

Listen how's the building coming along
Fine how would you like to have a beer
at my place

Anyone from Africa will tell you
a chicken head—
which shows you how a myth can wear away—
is hidden in the mud of every hut.

But now and then you read,
from France or Sweden,
about the trial of a builder
of skyscrapers for murder unexplained
of a good friend,
a wife or a child.

Sometimes still when buildings are torn down
we read of skeletons.

We always assume of course
falling into trouble
some casual tenant.

[handwritten annotation: that's our myth we assume]

For Rebecca, for Whom Nothing Has Been Written
Page after Page

We have a language that serves us more or less
for the earth and air and fire and the earth's water,
that sort of thing, for hydrogen and tin.

What phrase explains, what simile can guess,
a daughter's daughter? We half know who you are,
moment by moment, remembering what you were
as you grow past, becoming by quick revisions
an image in the door.

What matters when all the words are written and read
is what remains not said,
which is what long silences are for.

Professor

He sits in the room alone, imagines a storm
torn in strips from all the remembered storms
out of The Odyssey, The Ancient Mariner, Oz.
Somewhere inside the storm, a gray room
collects itself out of The House of Usher,
out of Beowulf and Dover Beach.
Two people are making love in the room,
throwing on the wall the flowering shadows
of all the remembered lovers, the terrible
and gentle remembered lovers, Sons and Lovers,
Paradise Lost, Padua, that little book
somebody passed around in the tenth grade
showing couples out of the comic strips
leading a second life. He sees out the window
the long-legged women of spring, taking walks.
He rolls them over his tongue. He thinks of names.
Anna Karenina. Moll Flanders. Blondie.

Green Mansions

There is an Amazon tribe that kills its children.

This tribe was only recently discovered.
Two hundred fifty are dead by white diseases.
They have decided to die by their own doing.

Every infant is blessed and fed and killed.
Summarily executed (this is Reuters).

They will be gone before the highway gets there
but there will be guides to explain it and you can drive by.

The Year They Outlawed Baseball

The year they outlawed baseball
nobody played.
The next year people said
how it used to be,
the center fielder leaping up the wall.
The next year a few men tossed a few
in backyards and basements
without the gloves.
The ball gives off a sound
hitting the leather
anyone around could recognize.
Still people talked
and that was the end of that.
For years the widows kept scarred and lopsided balls
on the top shelves of closets in back rooms
and thought of showing them to trusted friends.

The Last Person to Speak His Language Is Dying

Ways to say good-bye are going with him.

Words he said to his woman when she died
were long since said for the last time.
The nurse bends down.
"Do you hear me?"

He gives her the twenty syllables of summer.
She will be the last person to hear them.

"The fever," she says.

The Liberal Imagination

He knows how few people get to be
even if there seem to be a lot.
Every day he's pleased to be among them
but knows he wouldn't mind if he were not.

Main Street

We came here to live in a small town.
Already the bypass half encircles us.
The three-story houses on Maple Street are gone
except for one which is a funeral home
with sad blue blinking letters over the porch.

The streets are guarded by two-headed parking meters
which doesn't matter since half the stores closed down
after Sears and Penney's moved to the mall.

Now something neither town nor city takes over.
The hospital adds a wing. The census swells.
The city limits signs of six towns
move toward each other like suspicious children.

Our children whom we meant to raise as hicks
come strangely into the house and bring new words.
They are well bred and come from good stock.
They join us always for breakfast. We see in their eyes
and in their smiles they are patient and willing to wait.

Waiting for the Paper to Be Delivered

Late January.
Snow is on everything.
No matter how far I listen there is only silence.

Two yellow machines have worked for a week
cutting away the hill in front of the house
I have come to live in for the rest of my life.

On the highest part of the hill
one oak is standing.

Nothing else is vertical on the horizon.
It locks the white sky to the white earth.

Fly Me to the Moon

He learns what love can do and what it can't do.
He sees it in her face more than he wants to.

He recognizes the interrogative touch
he can't decipher and doesn't like too much.

Sometimes they do lie down together
and feel at home in the grace of one another.

This is not what he thought it would be,
but nothing else is, either. She would agree.

The Survivor

According to the helicopter pilot,
the staticky talk on the two-way radio,
the next crest and the next
up a dry wash a mile or so
and there: the tail fin first, a wing, unusual odors.
No one seems to be alive but a woman,
standing as still as the topless trees,
her left arm hanging loose in the crusted sleeve.

"What are your thoughts on being the sole survivor?"
says the reporter, stumbling beside the stretcher.

Says the lady, "Sir—," and then the stretcher slips
and she slides free and falls a hundred feet,
tumbling down the mountain, loosening rocks.

Some say the red ribbon she had in her hair
fluttered loose when she fell and was found
almost at once
by a large bird, white, or more gray than white.

The Well-Ordered Life

Once he went inside a pool hall.
The clicking billiard balls put him in mind
of African tribes who click to say, "I love you"
"What do you want?" "We're going to kill you, of course."
They skirted the circles of light in a secret frenzy.

He took his Instamatic every week
and thirty-five dollars to life class.
He didn't use film. He couldn't have hidden the pictures.
He circled and focused and framed. The breast and knee.
The purest art he said is the briefest art.

Once he hunted for love. A long time
he stood beside a little fat lady,
dressed in red, standing on the corner,
looking something like a fire hydrant.
She boarded a bus and left him there alone.

Daily the desperate ordering of this world,
the objects on his desk, the chosen words,
the knife, fork, and spoon, the folded napkin,
the one, two, three, the counting, counting,
a constant laying of sandbags on the levee.

Getting the Message

Hermes it was. Hermes with winged heels,
looking like an ad for FTD.
I woke to see his silhouetted frame
inside the window frame. Hermes it was.
With, I had to assume, a message for me.

He wore the same hard hat he always wore,
suggesting a nudist on a construction crew,
except the hat had wings. Except also,
he wasn't entirely nude. The ribbon flapped
and did precisely what it was meant to do.

Not meaning to seem a churl, a poor host,
or wanting to seem too easily surprised
by this event, this hour of the morning
here in a Houston hotel, and thus appear
outside of myth and thus uncivilized,

and on the other hand, not wanting to seem
so gullible as to think the man was there
if it should turn out later he never was,
I lay in a shape that may have been described
if I were standing up as devil-may-care.

The hat's wings fluttered once. He shifted the hat.
"My name," he said, "is Hermes." "I know," I said.
I figured I could give him credence enough
for a civil response, at which response he entered
and scooted my feet aside and sat on the bed.

He asked if I was me. I said I was,
but I was not the one about whom doubt
might naturally arise and did he suppose
I'd be convinced as easily as that.
"Convincing you is not what I came about."

The tone was matter-of-fact. "I have a message."
"I take it you do," I said, "if you're in fact
an entity." "I have a message for you
whether I'm an entity or not.
There's no need for rudeness." "So how do I act

when Hermes comes in the window? Understand,
I'm trying to keep a fix on what we call
the phenomenological world. It isn't easy."
"That's what the message is about," he said.
"I'll have to have your promise, first of all,

not to tell anybody about the visit."
"What possible difference," I said, "could it make to you?
Nobody would believe it." "No difference," he said.
"It's like the apple, or never looking back.
There has to be something you're not allowed to do."

"How do you know I'll do what I say?" I said.
"When I tell about it—were I to—
I'd know already what the message is."
"So you would," he said. "But in that case,
whatever I tell you turns out not to be true."

He plucked a quill and pulled from under his hat
a packet of papers. "If you would please sign here."
I signed the promise. He rose in a flurry of wings.
The message, in a swirling cursive, read,
What ought to happen happens in one year.

Mythic people like that sort of thing.
They tell you something that looks fine at first.
I've pondered it these past eleven months.
Now it's told, untold, there's nothing to tell.
Whatever it saved us from, or what it cost,
whether I lost us heaven, or spared us hell,
a die's uncast, a Rubicon uncrossed.

Ghosts

Some evenings, there are ghosts. There are. Ghosts
come in through the door when people come in,
being unable to open doors themselves
and not knowing (not knowing they are ghosts)

they could pass through anything, like thought.
They come and stand, move aimlessly about
as if each one of them had come to meet
someone who hadn't arrived. I always thought

of haunts and spirits as having a special power
like witches to do whatever they wanted to.
They don't. Pure energy without a cage
can do nothing at all. Whatever power

pushes or pulls the things of this world
to any purpose does it by piston or pistol,
mill wheel or spring or some such pushing back.
Spirit freed fades into the world.

Inertia, which is habit, holds their lines
a little while and then like memories
they weaken and fade. The glow is energy going.
They seem like actors trying to remember lines.

The trouble is they don't know they're dead.
We don't know very much about ghosts;
we think that some of those who aren't prepared
and die surprised don't understand they're dead.

They hang around. The kindest thing to do
if you should ever see one is simply to say,
"Listen, you're dead. You're dead. Get out of here."
That's what the ghost eventually will do

when we've told it again and again to go.
"Get out of here. Get out of here. You're dead."
They can't of course go anywhere on purpose;
you have to give them intent to make them go.

And who knows where? All this has to do
with Newton's laws. The figure disappears.
Somewhere there's a place. Be kind. Be firm.
Remember the only thing you have to do

is tell them the truth. Say, "You're dead. Get out."
Ignore the slow confusion on their faces.
Never pity. They can soak up pity.
Sympathy makes them denser and drags it out.

If pity comes, don't let it go to them.
Watch for a sudden change in temperature.
You still have a death to deal with.
Pity yourself, who could be one of them

to live—as it were—with all the embarrassment.
You would not want someone who sounds like
a movie director telling you you're dead.
Your tissue hands could not hide the embarrassment.

Late Show

Too tired to sleep I switch a picture on,
turn down the sound to let my attention drain.
A forest in summer. Dogs. A man is running.
It's starting to rain.

The man comes to a house. He breaks a window.
A girl getting out of the shower admiring herself
looks to see if the cat has knocked something
from the kitchen shelf.

She sees the man. She wraps a towel about her.
In the woods loosed from their leashes the dogs
are running in circles scratching at empty trees
sniffing at logs.

The woman is breathing behind a chair in the kitchen.
The man is leaning against the kitchen door.
Her mouth moves. He hits her in the face.
She falls to the floor.

He tears the towel away. He stands above her.
He looks a long time. He lets her curl
into a corner. Both of us can see
she is only a girl.

He takes her to her bed and drops her on it.
Looks at her as if he has not seen her
before now. Takes off his clothes and puts
himself between her.

He moves his lips. She bends her legs and locks him.
They move together. (I turn up the sound.)
They stop moving. They look in my direction.
A single hound

is crouping close. She shoves the man aside,
rolls out of bed, runs with nothing around her
into the rain, into the leaping dogs.
Lightning and thunder.

He sits on the bed, his back a slow curve.
Turn it off, he says, in God's name.
The door opens. A man with a long gun.
He takes aim.

Trying to Remember

You know in the muddy pond the fish is there.
It bumps the bait and late in the long shadows
it nudges a brief circle over the surface.
Give it up. It will die in the dark water.

The Ones That Are Thrown Out

One has flippers. This one is like a seal.
One has gills. This one is like a fish.
One has webbed hands, is like a duck.
One has a little tail, is like a pig.
One is like a frog
with no dome at all above the eyes.

They call them bad babies.

They didn't mean to be bad
but who does.

Form and Theory of Poetry

Think of how in a hurricane the winds
build up from nothing at all and suddenly stop
then start the opposite way and die down,
the way the traffic around a stadium
builds to the game, stops, starts again
going the other direction, dies down.
Think in the eye of a hurricane, then, of halftime.
At a football game, think of the Gulf Coast,
Biloxi, Mississippi, blown away.

Words

Strip to the waist and have a seat. The doctor
will be in soon. He smiles and the nurse smiles.
He sits on the table, bumping his knees together,
scratching around his navel, counting the tiles.

We never talk, she says, and so you talk
and everything you speak of falls apart.
This is how we come to understand
what they mean by chambers of the heart.

Some words are said to start a conversation.
Some, after which there's nothing more to say.
"Amen," for instance. "I said I was sorry."
"Tower, we're going down. This is PSA."

Style

Sometimes he would try to write a poem
and what he wanted to do was scribble circles
down one side of the page and up the other
and once he did but he knew it wasn't a poem
although there were those who would have called it one
assuming of course that it was done sincerely.

Not wanting to waste the paper or the time
and having a dean impressed by anything,
he titled it and signed it and sent it off
and there it was in the *Golden Rule Review,*
"Poem in Sincere Circles." It was sincere.
A few months later it got anthologized.

He sits at his desk devising variations,
starting in the center of the page,
circles in circles with small symbols in them.
He publishes everywhere and gets letters
asking for explanations he never gives.
Also he never gives readings anymore.

Believing in Symbols

1

One morning I put in the pocket of my shirt
not having put two and two together
a little calculator. That afternoon
it lay on my desk and turned out 8s for hours,
shorted through by those rippling shocks
the sinus node sends out, now beat, now beat.

So what do we say for science and the heart?
So with reason the heart will have its way?

Believing in symbols has led us into war,
if sometimes into bed with interesting people.

2

8 becomes in the time of solid state
the figure all the figures are made from,
the enabling number, the all-fathering 8;
1 through 7, also nothing and 9,
are all pieces of 8 which is only itself.

This makes a certain sense if you look at the sign
that says infinity, the Möbius strip,
a lazy 8 hung on the Gates of Heaven.

The pterodactyl, Pompeii, the Packard;
things take their turns. 3 and 7 are only
numbers again. Nothing stays for long.
Not to say that physics will ever fail us
or plain love, either, for that matter.
Like the sides of a coin, they may take turns,
or flipping fast enough, may seem to merge.

Call it, if you call it, in the air.
When the coin comes down, the tent comes down.
You look around, and there is nothing there.
Not even the planets. Not even the names of the planets.

Love and How It Becomes Important
in Our Day-to-Day Lives

The man who tells you which is the whiter wash,
the woman who talks about her paper towels,
the woman whose coffee holds her home together,
the man who smells the air in his neighbor's house,

the man who sings a song about his socks,
the woman who tells how well her napkin fits,
the man who sells the four-way slicer-dicer,
the woman who crosses tape between her tits,

and scores besides trample my yard, a mob
demanding to be let in, like Sodomites
yelling to get at my guests but I have no guests.
I crawl across the floor and cut the lights.

"We know you're there," they say. "Open the door."
"Who are you?" I say. "What do you want with me?"
"What does it matter?" they say. "You'll let us in.
Everyone lets us in. You'll see. You'll see."

The chest against the door begins to give.
I settle against a wall. A window breaks.
I cradle a gun in the crook of my elbow.
I hear the porch collapse. The whole house shakes.

Then comes my wife as if to wake me up,
a case of ammunition in her arms.
She settles herself against the wall beside me.
"The towns are gone," she says. "They're taking the farms."

Pity and Fear

In westerns the man who saddles up at night
is not going to say good-bye to someone
pretending to be asleep in the still cabin.

Which is to say he loves her and didn't mean to.
All she knows about him are dusty lies.
He stopped here to give his horse some water.

Or so he said. He stopped. It doesn't matter.
The man who saddles up his horse knows something.
What about her man? Will he not know?

Oh he will know, though he will never say it.
He will know his wife is not his woman.
He will become the sheriff and be a good one.

We see a passing of years. The man returns.
A windy desert town he barely remembers.
The tall son of the sheriff is dark and quick.

He gambles some. The women like him. His name
is Larry or Jim. He has his mother's eyes.
We know what will happen. Still we sit. We wait.

Evening: A Studio in Rome

The window here is hung in the west wall.
It lays on the opposite wall a square of light.
Sliced by the lopsided slats of the broken blind,
the light hangs like a painting. Now, and now,
the shadow of a swallow shoots across it.

I turn around to see the birds themselves,
scores of birds, hundreds, a thousand swallows.
I try to keep a single bird. I lose it.
In all that spinning not one bird spins loose.

I turn away from the window and back to work.
My eyes are caught again by the square of light.
I lean back in my chair and watch the picture
moving up the wall, the single birds
living out their lives in a frame of light,
until it touches the ceiling and fades out.
I turn around again and the swallows are gone.
The sun is gone. This minute Rome is dark
as only Rome is dark, as if somebody
could go out reaching toward it, and find no Rome.

The Woman in the Room

She stands at the foot of my bed and starts to speak,
pauses, looks confused and fades out,
the colors of pressed flowers, a sickly smell,
then nothing. A wide skirt once, a flowered blouse.
Pale naked once. The moon by daylight
has almost the color. The first time
she wore a blue gown. She had a rose
pinned to the waist, lace around her wrists.

Listen, Woman. Woman, I never loved you.
I'm not the man you remember. This may be the room.
The house has been here for generations.
If you could tell me what you're trying to say.

That's what I always say or something like it.
Or mean to. I don't say anything.
She opens her mouth and no sound comes out.
There isn't any air but the air she is.

Little by little I'm learning to read her lips.

From *The Boys on Their Bony Mules*

Children's Games

When the music is going strong
and everybody is marching along
you can bet he has put in his gray
hand and jerked a chair away.

He counts to seventy-five,
Oh, Love, if he plays fair,
but you can't take your time;
he may not go that far.

And when he lifts his head
and turns from side to side
he'll see our shirttails flapping
no matter where we hide.

Somebody leaves. You wonder where he goes.
The bottle spins and wobbles and comes to rest
pointing toward somebody on your right.
You grin inside yourself and feel blessed.
Now again the bottle spins and slows.

Predestination

The blind man gropes and our feet are frozen.
We lean away. We are not chosen,
we are stumbled on. How would it be
worse or better if he could see?

Learning

You sit by the bed
holding one of the disinterested hands.
You feel it lose its resistance.
It begins to cool.
Someone comes in and puts a hand on your shoulder.
You go home and make coffee.
You start to take off your clothes and you fall asleep.
The cup of coffee gets cold on the kitchen table.

Remembering the Man

Uneasy a February afternoon
we rode Indian Air, Calcutta to Delhi.
I leaned across and we looked out the window.
We saw a piece of Nepal, a perfect map.
Beyond Nepal half of the Himalayas
rose past all metaphor. A pot mender
looked up from his work to find us, shading his eyes.
"Look," you said. "There—the man looking up."
But we couldn't even see the sheep being driven
as slowly as always in front of the pot mender's tent
by his lazy brother-in-law who would certainly lose one
before a year was out to the ravenous wolves.

Standing Close to Greatness

His eyes shine like an expensive car.
His voice is distant and clear, like the Greek Islands.
We move around him as if someone
were writing his name all the time.
He forgives us our excessive love.

We do need the great ones, who brush their teeth
and never spit and who it is hard to think of
wanting a word.

O they are important for looking down as they do.
It is not true
that in the bathroom they act like anyone else.
They act great.

Still we know, we know,
for every object of universal acclaim
there must be others highly respected and fussy
who never heard the name
and snort and grumble when they tell us so.

Learning to Read

When I suspect I'm a character in a novel—
it's not all the time. Monday morning, for instance,
it's ten o'clock and people are wanting coffee
or I've been waiting a little too long for something,
a dentist, a beer, a bus,
I'm pretty sure I'm real. I buy the whole
ball as they say of wax.
When I suspect I'm being written is mostly
after dinner, the dark sun slipping away.
I'm sitting beside a window watching the sparrows
or watching the dogs tumble through the leaves
or the falling snow.
There's evidence enough, if you think about it:
the pride, the mounting tension,
the recognitions, an hour too late and useless,
the quick turns, the fortunate meetings,
the falling away of enemies and friends,
the obligatory scenes, the ritual candles
we throw before us against the resolving dark.

Going

The afternoon in my brother's backyard
when our mother in awful age and failing,
recognized as I came across the lawn
my dead father coming home for dinner,
what could I say? Come, give me your hand?
Let us walk together a little while?
Here it is 1915, we are married,
the first of our children is not yet born or buried,
the war in Europe is not yet out of hand,
the one you will not forget who wanted you first
is just as we are, neither old nor dead.
He still frets about us being together.

Good woman, wife, with five children to mourn for
and children arriving with children, what can I say?

See, we have come because we wanted to come.
Because of love. Because of bad dreams.
This is my wife. We live in another state.

The Man Who Believes in Five

is trying to find a way to get out of town.
People are running at him from all directions.

The woman who believed in two is dead
lying beside her cart at the supermarket.

The girl who wrote the report on the power of four
is naked and tied to a chair in the teachers' lounge.

The boy who turned his parents in for saying
one and six at meals has hanged himself.

Triplets are holy. A three-base hit is holy.
Tricorn hats are back in style again
and scholars study the trivial, digging deep.

Inference

The mouse
curling fur wet and warm
inside the belly of the owl
has been we might say born backward out of his life.

There is a man then who talks backward.
I mean he walks down the street moving his lips
and syllables fly into his mouth.
He could unsay die and the dead would rise,
day and the sun would go down.

Here though he has moved his mouth
and we are undone and distant,
love and touch
curled up and moist
in the little sacs of his lungs.

Rubaiyat for Sue Ella Tucker

Sue Ella Tucker was barely in her teens.
She often minded her mother. She didn't know beans
About what boys can do. She laughed like air.
Already the word was crawling up her jeans.

Haskell Trahan took her for a ride
Upon his motorbike. The countryside
Was wet and beautiful and so were they.
He didn't think she'd let him but he tried.

They rode along the levee where they hid
To kiss a little while and then he slid
His hand inside her panties. Lord lord.
She didn't mean to let him but she did.

And then she thought that she would go to hell
For having let befall her what befell,
More for having thought it rather nice.
And she was sure that everyone could tell.

Sunday morning sitting in the pew
She prayed to know whatever she should do
If Haskell Trahan who she figured would
Should take her out again and ask her to.

For though she meant to do as she was told
His hands were warmer than the pew was cold
And she was mindful of him who construed
A new communion sweeter than the old.

Then sure enough, no matter she would try
To turn her head away and start to cry,
He had four times before the week was out
All of her clothes and all his too awry.

By then she'd come to see how she had learned
As women will a lesson often earned:
Sweet leads to sweeter. As a matter of fact,
By then she was not overly concerned.

Then in the fullness of time it came to be
That she was full of child and Haskell he
Was not to be found. She took herself away
To Kansas City, Kansas. Fiddle-de-dee.

Fiddle-de-dee, she said. So this is what
My mother meant. So this is what I got
For all my love and whispers. Even now
He's lying on the levee, like as not.

She had the baby and then she went to the place
She heard he might be at. She had the grace
To whisper who she was before she blew
The satisfied expression from his face.

The baby's name was Trahan. He learned to tell
How sad his daddy's death was. She cast a spell
Telling how it happened. She left out
A large part of the story but told it well.

The Muse

poems about writing poems <meta-poem>

Driving south on U.S. 71
Forty miles from Fort Smith
I heard a woman speak from the backseat.
"You want a good idea for a closing line?"
I recognized the voice.
"Where did you come from?"
"I wiggled in back there when you stopped for gas.
You'd better pull over."
She knew about the cards I kept in my pocket
to scribble on whenever she came around.
We'd been through this before.
I bumped down from the blacktop and stopped the car.
Between a couple of oaks and a yellow line,
above the howl and sizzle of passing traffic,
she said some words. I waited. She looked out the window.
"Well?" I said. "Is that it?"
"It's all I have," she said. "Can't you do
anything for yourself?"
"I listen," I said. "That's what I'm supposed to do."
She took a slow breath and got out of the car.
"I'll try to get you something.
I'm going to walk around for a little while.
If you leave me here I'll forget I ever saw you."
"I won't leave you," I said. So I'm sitting here
between the darkening road and pin oak trees,
a 3 × 5 card in one hand, a pen in the other,
beginning to feel vulnerable and foolish
like a man waiting for more toilet paper
thinking he may have been left there and forgotten.

The Firebreathers at the Café Deux Magots

We sit at a sidewalk table.
Noilly Prat over ice.

A firebreather lost out of time,
his cheeks full of shadows,
takes off his shirt,
starts to spin it like a bullfighter's cape
and drops it.
He opens a blue plastic bottle,
soaks a torch, a broomstick wrapped in rags,
and waves the fire in front of him like a flag.

He seems to drink the alcohol like water.
He breathes in slowly.
He exhales a burning breath
red with yellow borders.

Flames run like liquid.
They drop in brief blazes from chin to chest.

With uncooperative hands and locked-in legs
he does this for nine silent minutes.
He bows like Pinocchio to the proper applause.
Aggressively among us he collects his coins.
His eyes when they come close
are bleary and small.
He seems to be drunk.
His hair is seared away.
His eyes don't have any lashes.
Blisters have shrunk into scars
on his chest and chin
like some exotic fruit left in the field.

One eye seems to be hunting
for something on its own.

He puts the plastic bottle
the torch and the cash
into a canvas bag and wanders away.
His feet sound like gravel poured on the pavement.

A woman plays a flute.
Her tall companion
long breasts moving like lovers
inside her blouse
comes and demands our money with great hands.

Another man,
years younger,
his green eyes lifting like fingers
the faces of women,
sheds his open shirt.

His chest is perfect and hard
and clean as marble.

Over the left nipple
one small round scar.

He opens the plastic bottle. He grins.
He tosses back the hair falling into his eyes
and then he makes a small move with his head,
a small, unconscious move,
the way one turns for a moment in mid-sentence
hearing a tumbler break in another room.

Lost in Ladispoli
for Ruth

Though we may never be seen alive again
by anyone who speaks English well
surely we are somewhere in Italy still
surely we are near the Mediterranean coast moving
by some definition
in this street-wise but halfhearted collapsible Fiat
through rutted mud between these narrow houses.

What the hell way is west?
They'll find us rusted shut, down a dead-end alley,
sitting up and obviously screaming at the end
like the people of Pompeii.

When suddenly here on a building
made from this mud
on a low flat roof a girl—
Who knows with these Italians?
Seventeen?—
tall in the warm morning sun in a blue bikini so brief
it barely repeats her mouth, her low-lidded eyes,
brushing out the long, the luminous hair.

She is more Roman this girl than all of Rome.

Her body turns as if the world were turning
(Sweet Love, how like you this?)
slowly as the Fiat fumbles,
churning the mud.

She raises an arm.
She may be stretching loose from the last threads of sleep.
She seems to be pointing to something.

We take the lane she shows us or seems to show us.

She gazes at us moving toward the sea
as if she has seen something remarkable
something that ought to be precisely remembered.
We stop and look back.
We gather her in
against the pull of gravity
and time
because
she has not yet heard
of either one.

In a Gradually Moving Car
Somewhere in Calcutta

The people filling the street
slide past the fenders of the car
and close in behind us,
eyes at the windows paying no attention
as if we were chugging along in a motor launch
up a river clogged with floating bodies.

No danger here, the driver says. No danger.

Rickshaw drivers don't have any shadows.
The sun falls through them onto the broken pavement.

A dog with no skin stands with stiff legs and trembles.

A woman washing her hair in the running gutter
raises her head for something that floats by.

A bride sits hard in the back of a black Buick
between solemn men like brothers.
Out of a nostril hangs a string of pearls.

The honking rises
one endless syllable
hosannah.

I think of an apple.

A one-legged boy in short black pants
hops out of an alley
as if all of us were cripples
dragging our second legs.

I think of an apple.

Two men who may be students
one wearing only a shirt
one wearing only the pants that belong to the shirt
make their almost unnoticed way
across the street,
their arms moving in quick, important ways.

The later babies, they take a hand or foot.
The driver tells me this. They beg better.
I know the driver is telling me driver's lies.
I pretend to believe him.
I frown, I shake my head.

Gray rags around her bones
a little girl crying
begins to balance her way along a rope
four feet above a clot of uncertain faces.
A woman
moves among the hands
collecting coins.

Barely above the heads
a dead man is borne on a board
riding the high hands of seven men.
He seems to be riding a narrow raft
down the same thick river.

I think of a single apple, dark,
with pale yellow markings around the stem,
resting in the middle of a small, round, walnut table.
A slender woman wearing a white dress,
touching the table lightly
with her long left hand
stands still and looks at the apple.
There is not a sound
except for one white curtain barely moved by the wind.

Normandy Beach

The waves on the Normandy coast jump heavily toward us.
Somewhere above the rolling, ocean-thick air
soldiers are lining up in a rising light.
The name we have come to find is whitely there.

We stand awhile above the ragged beach
where the German gunnery crews held hard
and spread the beach with bodies that still sprawl,
appearing and disappearing. A silent charge

comes out of the lifting fog, vague visions of men,
some of them drowning, some digging holes in the sand,
some lying on the sand with waves washing their boots.
We watch as the bodies fade away in the sun.

We find his name, Lieutenant, Arkansas.
To leave you there alone I turn around
to a curving monument, The Spirit of Youth
Rising Out of the Sea, what might be found

as frontispiece in a book of Romantic verse.
It must have suggested solace to someone:
arms that might be wings, and flowering waves,
what Shelley as a sculptor might have done.

I watch the statue standing over the stones
and think of what the living do to the dead.
Then suddenly what you came to do is done.
We stop in a dark store for cheese and bread

and a bottle of wine. We find that famous room
where tapestry runs like a frozen picture show
the slow invasion that went the other way
over eleven hundred years ago,

princes and knights and horses in feathers and metal
changing the names of things. An iron cross
leans from an iron gate at the foot of a hill
where careful Germans step out of a touring bus.

I don't want to make a bad metaphor here
and everything is suddenly metaphor.
We head the Fiat south in a sundown light
and follow the back roads. Beside a river

we make the wine outlast the food and sit still
and watch the water run. Thought after thought
comes into my head and goes. Lonely companion,
there's something I have to tell you but I don't know what.

Aesthetic Distance

The moon is dark. We have our drinks on a terrace
on Gianicolo hill. There is a little war
in the streets of Rome. We see the flashes from pistols,
the sweeping lights, we hear the pistols popping.
We watch a Molotov cocktail burning its curve.
"Star bright," somebody says. "Make a wish."

For Victor Jara

MUTILATED AND MURDERED
THE SOCCER STADIUM
SANTIAGO, CHILE

This is to say we remember. Not that remembering saves us.
Not that remembering brings anything usable back.

This is to say that we never have understood how to say this.
Out of our long unbelief what do we say to belief?

Nobody wants you to be there asking the question you ask us.
There had been others before, people who stayed to the end:

Utah and Boston and Memphis, Newgate, Geneva, Morelos—
Changing the sounds of those names, they have embarrassed us,
     too.

What shall we do with the stillness, do with the hate and the pity?
What shall we do with the love? What shall we do with the grief?

Such are the things that we think of, far from the thought that you
    hung there,
Silver inside of our heads, golden inside of our heads:

Would we have stayed to an end or would we have folded our faces?
Awful and awful. Good Friend. You have embarrassed our hearts.

Auf Wiedersehen

[handwritten: Auf]

[handwritten: — UNTIL WE MEET AGAIN —]
[handwritten: x SEEING AGAIN x]
[handwritten: x free verse x]
[handwritten: + iambic pentameter]

When open trucks with German prisoners in them
passed in convoy through the small town
I dreamed in, my fourteenth year, of touchable breasts
and cars and the Cards and the Browns, we grabbed the shirts
we twisted and tied for bases and chased the trucks
past all our houses slow as we could run.

We tossed the baseball up to one of the guards
who sometimes pretended to keep it but threw it back.
Once I threw it badly. A German caught it.
A boy barely older than I was and blonder
and nearly as thin. He grinned and I thought how much
the baseball belonging to John Oscar Carpenter
must have cost. The guard didn't seem concerned
about the baseball or me. We ran for blocks
behind the flatbed truck. The side rails rattling
made the same sense the Germans did
calling and tossing the ball to one another.

We ran in silence needing our breath to breathe
and knowing that begging raises the value of things.
At the edge of town the convoy speeded up.
Everyone stopped but me and the truck pulled away.
I looked back once to see the seven others
standing on the curb of the last street
loose and surprised as a group on a picnic
looking into a river where someone has drowned.

When I turned back to the trucks, pumping my arms,
the pain in my side coming to punish me hard,
to burn the blame away and make us even,
even John Oscar Carpenter and I,
the young German hauled back and let the ball
fly in a flat arc from center field.
I caught it. I held it in the hand I waved
as truck by truck the convoy shifted gears.
"Wiedersehen," he yelled. A word I knew.
I turned and pegged the ball to home in time.
I wondered if he had killed the Rogers boy
or thrown the hand grenade at Luther Tackett
that blew his arm away. I had done something
nobody ever had done. It was large and frightful.
We walked in amazement awhile and went to our houses.

Your grandchildren, German, do they believe the story,
the boy in Arkansas, blonder than you?

We

We are pleased to present for your listening pleasure . . .
This is Civil Defense for your own good.
Stay in your houses. This is not a test.
Something is moving barely above the trees
at the edge of the city coming in from the south.
Stay away from the windows. Turn off all lights.
If you have been caught in your car pull over and stop.
Tons of darkness are falling out of its eyes.
From every hole something resembling something
dribbles down. It glistens on the grass.
It has a certain cast. It smells like something.
It's one of ours, it's one of ours. It's all right . . .
the Second Piano Concerto in B-flat.

A Newspaper Picture of Spectators at a Hotel Fire

At three in the afternoon on a clear day
fire breaks out in a tall St. Louis hotel
on the sixteenth floor and takes it from end to end.

That is how high above this street of faces
as fixed as stones three women stood in windows
with cracking glass behind them till one by one
they tested the air like swimmers and stepped stiffly out.
They come down with zeroes in their mouths.

One among the watchers has turned his back
on such important people who step into nothing,
who kick their way to the curb, to the tops of cars.
He takes away what he wants, the negative faces.

All morning we are moody. We mention the picture,
the long, slow arms, the women falling toward us.

The Story

In a small town in the mountains they tell of a man
who started showing up in pictures of weddings,
of softball teams and picnics, a dozen years
after he was sealed and weighted down
by a quarter ton of dry mountain dirt.
His friends were Christian people full of faith.
Some took his face at first as an omen of evil,
some as a sign of favor. When nothing happened
of any special sort in a couple of years
it came to be seen as more a rude intrusion,
something they had to learn to live with
like the smell of the paper mill.
                              It was commonly held
that he was haunting the town for private reasons.
Not knowing where those reasons were likely to take him,
some people started undressing in the dark.
Twice the town council in something like secret
hired men who said they could make him go away.

One built a fire and burned hair from the barbershop.
One threw the preacher's cat off the Baptist church.
When pictures of these events came out in the paper,
the dead man was there in the crowd, with wide eyes.

Then one day in a shot of a prize hog
at the county fair, five years from the first appearance,
he wasn't there. Some said the burning hair
had worked exceeding slow; some said, the prayers;
some said the cries of the cat had finally done it.

Lovers began to look at each other again;
women took their magazines back to the bathroom.
People wondered what made him go away
as much as they wondered once what brought him back.

The only people who did not seem concerned
were Mary Sue Tattersall and her husband, Edward,

who ran the seed store at the edge of town,
kept two cows and some chickens, went to bed early,
and Saturday mornings took long walks in the woods.

Documenting It

First he could not remember
where T. S. Eliot said,
"Between the plan and the act falls the shadow"
or if what he said was plan or something else.
This bothered him so that he thought of cutting back
to one or two martinis after supper.

Second he forgot
why he had driven down to the grocery store.
He sat in the parking lot for ten minutes.
Why did I drive down to the grocery store?
He went home and fixed himself a drink
and waited for his wife to ask where the soap was.

Third he could not remember
what class he was teaching,
Comparative Physiology, Biology I,
or something he had forgotten how to do.
He thought of those dreams of final examinations
in classes he registered for but never attended,
meant to but never did, couldn't find out
where it was meeting until the day of finals.
He had to go and look at the awful questions.

He found that when he panicked he was aroused.

He prayed but it did not help. It doesn't always.

Running into Things
for twelve in their pickup trucks

As lemmings run into the sea, old priests appear
at the house of Thomas Aquinas and Thomas More
to fix their faith and Hume opens the door.
They ran that way before the sea was there.

Because they couldn't remember the bypass
that cut across their roads and cut them down
a dozen farmers have died coming to town.
All they remembered was dust, gravel, and grass.

Rock

For two days I have dug around a rock
that may have been buried where it was
to hold the county in place.

I am building in front of my house
a wall of fieldstones.

Every two hours I say
I have earned a beer.

All of this afternoon
I have rolled this barely
round and enormous rock
up a gradual hill
to a place prepared
in my lonely and useless wall.

Four times the rock has pulled away
out of the crying grip of my arms and knees
and rolled back to the hole it lay in forever.

I know enough to know when to feel important.

I try to give my mind to something else.
I imagine I may be forgiven for living in town
with two dogs that don't know how to hunt
because this hurts like manhood and my hand is bleeding.

I stop and look at the blood.

I try to give my mind to something else.

It's you and I against the world my love.
The world is
I have to tell you
a prohibitive favorite.

Up there is a fence with a hole the size of this stone.
Here is a house where I live with a better woman
than I had meant to be with and two dumb dogs.

I have earned more beers than I can drink.

The woman across the street
will be naked tonight
stepping out of the bathtub
reaching for something.

My knees are gone.
It's getting late, she says.
You ought to come in.

I guess I should, I say but look at the rock.

It really is big, she says. I don't see how you did it.

Sisyphus my friend
what does forever mean?

I go into the house. She hands me a mug of beer.

Here, unlike forever, it is six o'clock.
The big hand and the little hand, they tell us.

Trying

The husband and wife had planned it for a long time.
The message was folded into a paper boat.
The children were all asleep. In the backyard
they put the boat in the pool. We are here. Save us.

Rebecca at Play

She lies in the grass and spreads her golden hair
across the grass, as if in simple joy
at being what she is, quietly aware
that she is not a tree or horse or boy.

Logos

In the beginning that unbroken breath
the endless exhalation
was broken by the terrible mercy
of God's own tongue, God's teeth,
into one round verb.
Its offspring number so many
nobody could count them.

Words are shadows, words are only shadows.
We take them for more than shadows. They seem to be more.
They enlist in the armies of our poems.
They quiet unhappy lovers and name our children.
They join all things together and put them asunder.
People send them out with clear directions,
Mean this, Mean that.
They undo whatever they do as soon as they do it.
Hush.

I press the remote control.

A jazz quintet is reinventing music.
They play with calm and perfect concentration.
There are no words in the world,
except for the word of God:
Let there not be words,
Let there be a magnificent moving of fingers,
Let there be reeds and brass,
Let there be piano, bass, and drum.
Da-biddely-biddely-biddely-biddely
Bump.

Ah, but we know, don't we?
A waiter can hear you make that sound all day
and never will bring you a cheese sandwich
no matter how badly you want one.

In the beginning was F-sharp.

That would have been a very different story.

People

When people are born
we lift them like little heroes
as if what they have done
is a thing to be proud of.

When people die
we cover their faces
as if dying were something
to be ashamed of.

Of shameful and varied heroic things we do
except for the starting and stopping
we are never convinced
of how we feel.
We say oh, and well.

Ah, but in the beginning
and in the end.

***Paying Some Slight Attention to His Birthday
the Associate Professor Goes about His Business
Considering What He Sees and a Kind of Praise***

Standing in front of my students,
a careful man,
I hear one tumbler turn.

The students are sitting still in their one-armed chairs
like rows of slot machines,
most surely come to rest
on the wrong combinations.

I have not helped them very much.

I love them. I tell them the truth:

The underside of the soul is rough to the touch.

The smell of the armpits of angels
is like the sound of tomatoes,
the falling of pickles.

It's easier to find the smallest needle
than prove there's not one hidden in the haystack.

For a sonnet you put two limericks together
and one verse of "The Old Rugged Cross."

Now it is suppertime. I have done my job.

The sun coming down makes me feel sad and contented,
like finding the house of your life ten years ago,
another car in the driveway,
the crepe myrtle gone.

A dog drops at my feet again and again
a rubber ball to be thrown across the grass.

All of my children have loved me
more than they might have
and in their own skins do love me still.

Across the road a cow
settles into the grass
or the sun
settles into the grass like a casual cow,
slow and heavy and full to its simple face
with the unquestionable rightness of being a cow
or the sun
whichever it is going down into the grass
this suddenly silent hour, this year come round.

In Nashville, Standing in the Wooden Circle Sawed Out from the Old Ryman Stage, the Picker Has a Vision
for Tom T.

I'll tell you what it was. I thought about those
who suddenly came on lines they couldn't cross over—
Hank and Patsy and Hawkshaw and Gentleman Jim
and all the others who did what they did and are gone,
John Keats and Wilfred Owen and Jimmie Rodgers.

Standing a misplaced man in that crowded space
with nobody breathing but me, I had nothing to say.
My head was full of words from those good pickers
about our lives and the lives they take us to.
Lord, the years of wine and city lights.

I thought of the small square of the planet Earth
I say I own, of my ridiculous self
pacing it off drunk at four in the morning
trying to understand what a place is worth.

It's a long time gone that we stopped counting things;
neither of us is going to die young.
Still fish grow fat, they lay their eternal eggs,
full grow the breasts and long the slender legs
of the young women we watch and forget about.

I heard it said by a woman in full sun
who only tells her lies from dusk till dawn
that nothing guards heaven or hell; it's the days to come
in this plain world without us we can't get through to.

I tell you, Tom, they will not let us pass.
Madness, Old Age, and Death, the rough boys
who come down from the hills on bony mules
know where we mean to go and they mean to stop us.
They make a line in the dirt and stand there.
Madness we can deal with. We know his moves.
And Death's a sissy; he never comes full face
when he's all by himself. He sneaks about. He hides.
Old Age is slow but he never stops to rest.
He can chase us down like a schoolyard bully
and sit on our chests until we barely breathe
while Death creeps close to put out his fist and hit us.

So what do we do, Tom? I'll tell you what.
We take our breaths and loves to let them go
and tell the names of things to the forgetful air.

Sir

(ONE OF THE PRESIDENT'S PEOPLE HAS SOMETHING TO SAY
JANUARY 20, 1981)

In the first world we know there is only the present.
Nothing was or will be. Then only the future.
Then only the past, and then we are the past.

This we understand is the nature of things.

Still, when Time falls in to fill the places
our unaccountable hands have hollowed out,
we, being who we are, will flail against it
because we have not done what we meant to do,
because there has not been much that we understood
and the little we learned returned us to where we started.

This may also be in the nature of things.

We have dreamed of honor and the forthright heart
as persons blind from birth imagine light,
have barely begun to find the uses of love,
have learned to speak of that giving and greedy God
who is the earth and will not forgive us always,
into whose mouths we have lowered our fathers and mothers
and children forever. He is jealous and knows our names.

History stands, like a sad teacher, beside us,
waiting to lay a ruler across our backs
to say again that we have answered wrongly.

What we wanted to do we have not done
but we have done a hard thing to do.
Love (this most worn word) we have not understood;
on rare days, even so, we have used it well.

What we wanted to do we have not done
but we have done the longest thing to do.

This is not to commemorate an end.

What have we done? Sir, we have done right.
Right once done, there is no ending to it.

Some Lines Finished Just before Dawn
at the Bedside of a Dying Student
It Has Snowed All Night

The blind from birth, they do not know
that roads diminish as they go
away from us. They know that in
our later years the hair grows thin.
They know it sometimes goes away.
They do not know it turns to gray.
They do not know what mirrors are.
They do not comprehend the dark
any better than the light.
They may recognize the night
as chill and a change in how things sound
and how we gather inside the house.
They do not know the way they cast
their morning shadows toward the west.
They have to trust that moon and star
are something as we say they are.
They cannot know with certainty,
whatever we say, that we can see.

Some physicists believe in four
planes of space. This is more
than we can know, lacking the sense
to see the plane our reason bends
about the other three. This
is not called faith. That's what it is.

Confessing faith, had we as well
let in God and heaven? And hell,
fastened as it is to heaven?
So the soul becomes a given,
given heaven and hell and Him?
And cherubim and seraphim?
Ghosts and ogres? Vampires? Elves?
People who can turn themselves
to cats and make potatoes rot
and curdle a mother's milk? Why not?

This man with tubes is going to die
today, tonight, tomorrow. I,
I, I, I . . . How good
that sounds to me. If I could,
would I take his place? I don't
have to answer and I won't.
But I am angry at the snow
caught in the car lights. We don't know,
though we watch him, what he will do,
don't know if he is passing through
a wall or running into one,
to fall together, all of him done.

uncertainty of death

In either case we say good-bye
mostly with our eyes and try
to be exactly here, to watch
beside him while he dies, with such
an ease it seems we mean to go
beside him all the way. And so
we do. As far as we can see.
That says less than it seems to say.
Already the light when I turn that way
is dim. Sometimes I see the shapes
of people flying. Or clouds, perhaps.
Or trees. Or houses. Or nothing at all.

These are the thin thoughts you call
to the front of my mind. It's a feathery three
o'clock in the morning. We've gotten through
almost another measured night.

There's love to serve and sufficient light
in the living mode. I wish you would stay.

The nurse will disturb you soon. I will say
good morning again. I will mention the snow.
I will lie about this. I will get my coat
and tie my shoes. I will stop and stand
by the bed awhile and hold your hand
longer than you like for me to
and drive home dying more slowly than you.

In Another Town

Out of a sealed window
in a bookless room where I have stayed too long
I see a man and a woman standing on a bridge.
I wonder why they are there this hour of the morning.
They grip the railing.
I suppose they are trying to solve a problem.
They leave without touching and walk in different directions.
Daylight takes over the bridge cable by cable.
If someone were to come now and knock on the door
I would say, "Look how sunlight collects on the bridge."

Living on the Surface

The dolphin
walked upon the land a little while
and crawled back to the sea
saying something thereby
about all that we live with.

Some of us
have followed him from time to time.
Most of us stay.
Not that we know what we're doing here.

We do it anyway
lugging a small part of the sea around.
It leaks out our eyes.

We swim inside ourselves
but we walk on the land.

What's wrong, we say, what's wrong?

Think how sadness soaks into
the beds we lie on.

Jesus, we've only just got here.
We try to do what's right
but what do we know?

From *Imperfect Love*

On Seeing Projected Figures
for War Dead in the Twentieth Century

No age was less assured a heaven waits
to welcome home the souls it liberates,
or ever so proficient as our own
at freeing them from bondage to the bone.

Politics

Mowing the lawn, having done with a tangle
of briar, with hornets buzzing in the eaves,
he is imposing order, but he leaves
some ragged grass where fences make an angle,
trapping a small shadow most of the day.
There, in the swarming morning, circling twice,
his dog turns herself intently clockwise
then drops on the flattened grass. In this way
she reshapes the world to suit a hound.
A square yard of his yard he leaves to her
because he sees that both of them are bound
as Jesus, Jefferson, and Caesar were
(as all people are, and some small friends)
to change a stubborn world to fit their ends.

Stopping to Look at a Crèche
in a Jewelry Store Window

Burros, taken to Death Valley by prospectors
and lost in the desert, by eating the few grasses
and other green things that grew there, caused the death
of wild goats that lived there and other animals.
But they don't know they did that, being asses.

Or so we've assumed, but seeing them gathered round
the portable manger of Bethlehem, with angelic features,
bowed heads, and bending knees, one has to wonder
what they know of guilt and innocence,
these beasts of burden, these simple, braying creatures.

One Day a Woman

One day a woman picking peaches in Georgia
lost her hold on the earth and began to rise.
She grabbed limbs but leaves stripped off in her hands.
Some children saw her before she disappeared
into the white cloud, her limbs thrashing.
The children were disbelieved. The disappearance
was filed away with those of other women
who fell into bad hands and were soon forgotten.
Six months later a half-naked man in Kansas
[working on the roof of the Methodist church]
was seen by half a dozen well-known
and highly respected citizens to move
directly upward, his tar brush waving,
until he shrank away to a point and vanished.
Nobody who knew about the first event
knew of the second, so no connection was made.
The tar brush fell to earth somewhere in Missouri
unnoticed among a herd of Guernsey cows.

One of Those Rare Occurrences on a City Bus

For exactly sixty seconds riding to work
approaching a traffic light going to green
he understands everything. I mean from the outer
curling edge of the universe to quarks,
the white geometries of time, of language,
death and God, the potted plants of love.
He sits there and looks at the truth. He laughs.
What could we want, except for him to laugh?
Understanding all, he understands
he has only sixty seconds, then he returns
to live with us in ignorance again,
and little enough to laugh at. "Do you have a pen,"
he says to the man beside him,
"that I could use?" The man pats his pockets
and shakes his head and shows his open palms
to say that he is sorry. Fifty-three. Fifty-four.

Mecanic on Duty at All Times

The license plate was another state and year.
The man's slow hands, as if they had no part
in whatever happened here, followed the hollows
and hills of his broad belt. Inside the car
four children, his face again, with eyes like washers,
were as still as the woman, two fingers touching her cheek.
"How much?" he said. "Well maybe fifty dollars
if I can find a used one. I guess I can."
The hands paid no attention. Out in the sun
light wires dipped and rose and dipped again
until they disappeared. *Flats Fixed* and *Gas*
and *Quaker State* squeaked in the wind. Just that.
And the speeding trucks, wailing through their tires.

Divorce

A man existed for seventeen spidery years
in the crawl space under the rafters of his home.

His Ford was found on a bridge.
His wife stood on the slick riverbank
shifting from foot to foot
as if she had gone there with the wrong congregation.

That was when he slipped into the house.

He came down by night and took some food.
Only enough so nobody would notice.

In two or three years he learned to tell by sound
like a blind man what happened in the rooms beneath him.

He heard the children grow up as the music changed.
The girl was a Brownie Scout for a little while
and then the phone began to ring all day.
The boy let the screen door slam till he graduated.

Sometimes his wife would bring a man home.
He understood everything,
the shutting of the door,
the stumbling in the dark,
the quietness that occupied the house.

Animals

I think the deaths of domestic animals
mark the sea changes in our lives.
Think how things were, when things were different.
There was an animal then, a dog or a cat,
not the one you have now, another one.
Think when things were different before that.
There was another one then. You had almost forgotten.

After a Brubeck Concert

Six hundred years ago, more or less,
something more than eight million couples
coupled to have me here at last, at last.
Had not each fondling, fighting, or fumbling pair
conjoined at the exquisitely right time,
thirty-four million times, I would be an unborn,
one of the quiet ones who are less than air.
But I will be also, when six hundred years have passed,
one of seventeen million who made love
aiming without aiming to at one
barely imaginable, who may then be doing
something no one I know has ever done
or thought of doing, on some distant world
we did not know about when we were here.
Or maybe sitting in a room like this,
eating a cheese sandwich and drinking beer,
a small lamp not quite taking the room from the dark,
with someone sitting nearby, humming something
while two dogs, one far away, answer bark for bark.

A Poem for Emily ← grand daughter

Small fact and fingers and farthest one from me,
a hand's width and two generations away,
in this still present I am fifty-three.
You are not yet a full day.

When I am sixty-three, when you are ten,
and you are neither closer nor as far,
your arms will fill with what you know by then,
the arithmetic and love we do and are.

When I by blood and luck am eighty-six
and you are someplace else and thirty-three
believing in sex and God and politics
with children who look not at all like me,

sometime I know you will have read them this
so they will know I love them and say so
and love their mother. Child, whatever is
is always or never was. Long ago,

a day I watched awhile beside your bed,
I wrote this down, a thing that might be kept
awhile, to tell you what I would have said
when you were who knows what and I was dead
which is I stood and loved you while you slept.

The Vanishing Point

Often I squinted my courage to see the spot
where all lines converge, but only saw
my father before it, spreading like a tree.

He is diminished now into that unplace
where there is nothing, neither breath nor breadth,
and I have felt a generation move.

I am standing, it seems all of a sudden,
with no one now between that point and me,
sliding toward it slowly as I can.

I grieve to celebrate. And may my children,
back down the widening years, see before them
some such old and serviceable simile.

On a Photograph of My Mother at Seventeen

How come to town she was, tied bright and prim,
with not a thought of me nor much of him.

Now, tied to a chair, she tries to pull free
of it and the world. Little is left of me,

I think, or him, inside her teetering head
where we lie with the half-remembered dead.

Her bones could be as hollow as a bird's,
they are so light. Otherness of words.

They could be kite sticks. She could be a kite;
that's how thin her skin is. But now some light

from somewhere in the brain comes dimly through
then flickers and goes out. Or it seems to.

Maybe a door opened, where other men
and women come and go, and closed again.

How much we need the metaphors we make
to say and still not say, for pity's sake.

Villanelle

19 line poem
<poem>
2 alternating
✱ 2 lines ✱

For Lucinda, Robert, and Karyn

I leave you these, good daughters and honest son,
(to have or toss away)
when all is said and done:

Undercuts

a name that rocks like a boat; some thoughts begun;
a fondness for instruments/I didn't play.
I leave you these, fair daughters and far son:

134

a sense of the probable (the one
sure anchor for the brain); a place to stay
as long as it stands. When all is said and done

you'll share the glory I won, or might have won,
for things I said or things I meant to say.
I leave you these, tough daughters and rocky son:

a tick no springs or brain or batteries run;
the valley in the mattress where I lay.
When all is said and done,

I'll leave my unpaid debts to everyone,
a slow love and resentment's sweet decay.
I'll leave you to yourselves, my daughters, my son,
when what's to say and do has been said and done.

Sunset: The Canary Islands

What are we to do with this hour of the evening
when the curving distinction between the sky and the sea
is almost gone
and the waves breaking white on the dark shore
and falling back
sound like the steady breathing of some long creature
sleeping or waiting?

In a small house high above the water
smiling for no reason I can name
you pick up a deck of cards and begin to shuffle.
We are both pleased by the riffle of the shuffling cards
which is not like any other sound.

135

Entropy

You say hello and part of what you spend
to say it goes to God. There is a tax
on all our simplest thoughts and common acts.
It will come to pass that friend greets friend
and there is not a sound. Thus God subtracts
bit by little bit till in the end
there is nothing at all. Intend. Intend.

*My Wife Reads the Paper at Breakfast
on the Birthday of the Scottish Poet*

Poet Burns to Be Honored, the headline read.
She put it down. "They found you out," she said.

A Little Poem
for Jack Marr

We say that some are mad. In fact
if we have all the words and we
make madness mean the way they act
then they as all of us can see

are surely mad. And then again
if they have all the words and call
madness something else, well then—
well then, they are not mad at all.

One of the Crowd on the Shore Tells How It Was

Mark 5:1–17

"What a wonderful thing has come to pass,"
everyone said. It was some day, all right,
for him set free of demons, and his kin.
All of them were Christians after that.
At first the people cheered and clapped their hands.
"Jesus!" they said. "Did you see what he did?"
Except, of course, the owners of the hogs.
I can tell you they had some things to say,
with two thousand pigs running amok.
"The whole damn business gone, the years of work!
How we gonna feed our wives and kids?
Someone's gonna pay for this, by God.
Who the hell does this man think He is?"
After a while this made the crowd uneasy
and then they got to grumbling, nervous-like.
Finally they told the man to leave
but when His boat was almost out of sight
there were the owners, yelling through their hands,
"What are you going to do about our pigs?"

speculative

belief behind skepticism

capitalistic society *

Tearing Down the Hotel

They are tearing down the oldest hotel
in Spring Lake, New Jersey. People sat here
in wicker chairs, reading Henry James,
when women wore long dresses and high shoes
and talked to men in hard straw hats and blazers
of motorcars and Egypt. Out of their sight,
men with large hands and unbreakable words
complained to women who never slept enough.

People came here when men in medicine wagons
sold bottles of dark elixir to women who waited
in small, fictitious towns, in houses with fringes,
rocking upstairs for days, the last drop gone.

Cars and aeroplanes and moving pictures,
adventures of goggles and boots, made here once
a surety as bright as a pale wine
caught by candlelight and nearly as brief.
Then they died, but that was different, too.
They died knowing that love by vulgar love,
barring only the yawn of a God grown bored,
eternal generations would bloom above them.

When the structure someone supposes here
to take the place of this hollow hotel
is pulled apart, say in a hundred years,
someone will say, maybe, thinking of us:
they were like this and that, read such and such;
they talked of these matters in those old chairs;
they never quite believed that we would be here
recalling the dead, pulling their buildings down.

The Promotion

We are not a large concern, although compared
to what the firm was when my uncle chose
to let it run itself, we are not small.
I'm glad you both could come. Let me freshen those.
I do not mean to denigrate my uncle,
whose seed this was. No growth, not a hundredfold,
can match the making of something out of nothing.
I give him his due, but he was losing hold
when I had nothing but hold. His mind and body
both would wander. My first day, I thought
he might not outlast another clean shirt.
He would go home at noon, but still he taught
me half of what I know. I never suffered
much of an education. I lived in the hills.
I brought a small embarrassment to my uncle
and then a threat and then a battle of wills.
I knew as much as a dog does about Sunday
but I had an ease in speaking. Anyway,
you can't fall out of a well, so I took chances.

Soon my uncle was staying home all day.
I know you've heard I took this company over
by untoward means. This is purely falsehood.
It took no cunning at all—only some courage
and a sense of the differences in right and good
consistent with a changing situation.
That's a Magritte that seems to have caught your eye.
I hope I haven't bored you. Please help yourselves;
my wife made all of these. Then by and by
I had to let my young cousin go.
His father lived in the past; this one carried
the future around with him. He never believed
much in the present world. And then he married
a scarce-hipped woman. You know the kind of girl
that cooks turnips and peas in the same pot,
the kind that gets entailed in her man's affairs.
The kind of woman yours is clearly not.
You can trust a high-breasted woman.
Small women getting undressed will lay their rings
in patterns and turn their stockings right side out,
but this has no effect on the order of things.
Then there was my son, born to my first wife,
a woman with all the qualities of a hound
except loyalty. When he was grown
he smelled the bread and came scratching around.
I gave him the chance you have to give a son
even though this one, born of his mother, lied
so bad his wife had to call the dog.
I'm not at home with words. Believe I tried.
When I saw he couldn't do the job
I offered him the southwest territory.
He's somewhere selling shoes. His wife left him
with nothing but a note. That's a story
I'll tell you sometime when you care to hear it.
A man needs a woman with no disdain
for what the man is, or he has no center
and spends his time in foolishness and pain.
I need a man with pride in what he is not,
a man with simple habits I can trust,
who wants just barely more than what he's got,

who'll do me in if he can, or wait if he must.
But that's enough. My wife is giving the sign
that I must light the candles and choose the wine.
What is your pleasure?

A Summer Afternoon
an Old Man Gives Some Thought
to the Central Questions

Grass grows out of every sidewalk crack.
Briars have taken the garden.
The arteries of the old dog harden almost audibly.
The basement door is broken and the mice are back.

So this is how things are: this face
that doesn't belong to anybody,
a lot of things I ought to throw away,
the grass that knew its place.

I overdramatize somewhat. There's nothing bricks,
a hoe, some putty, nails, and luck can't fix.
Almost everything is redeemable.
The dog and I are not.

Time sometimes heals the mind
and the metaphorical heart
but ravages all the while the bones and the hair
and the poor, sad, fleshy part.

But this is something we have understood.
This was part of the deal our parents made
back in the very beginning of the dream.

I picked up a young bird yesterday
that I thought was dead.
I was going to throw it away
then one of the delicate gray lids lifted.
The eye was as large
as if a child had drawn it.
It knew me with total recognition
as a thing that would have its way.

The way a dying man
his leg in a bear trap too long
might hear either a bear or a man
coming toward him
and listen with some interest.

So it is at the end,
but who would want to be an old house
who, being hammered on all day,
understood nothing?

On a Trailways Bus a Man Who Holds His Head Strangely Speaks to the Seat Beside Him

I brought a book to make the time pass.
It's nothing but another boring thriller.
The people in it, they don't like it either.
We're going to change the whole thing around.
You ought to read it when we get it done.

It's hard to be in a book, living a life
somebody else made up, doing things
you don't like to do, starting your life
halfway through a meal, or driving to work.
Also sometimes the print is very small.

So, anyway, if the girl across the aisle
should brush her hair back, like this, or smile
in such a way as says she wants attention,
I wish that you would trade places with her.
I have more attention than most people.

I can give her any amount she wants.
Not that it will change much for me.
I've got the only future I'm going to have.
But bless me, Lord, I could have been born
somewhere else where no one speaks English.

There are places that even those that live there
never heard of, places with dictators
that force democracy on everybody
and people are poor and dumb and ride donkeys.
Lord love us all, we don't know what we do.

I needed so much to do something well
after yesterday and the day before,
I thanked a woman twice and kissed her hand
because she said I was a perfect stranger.
People have loved and left and no one remembers.

The window here could be a clock, Lord love us,
the way the fields fly by. Sometimes I pray
to be here for whatever happens next
and hope that if it's good it happens twice
or lasts a long time.

Schumann Adds Trombones to His Second Symphony
after Mendelssohn Conducts the First Performance

I'm getting better but Mendelssohn was right.
I don't have the strength to stand there
weaving all those colors into something
no one has heard before, in front of people
who know that I went mad and suppose I am.
He was a good friend to take my place
and point the applause to me. Writing it down
took an inordinate time. Darkness fell
one quiet Sunday morning for six months.
I finished it, which ought to say something.
It hurt me not to conduct the first performance,
but there was a blessing in it. All these years
I never had a chance to stand back
and see a work the way another sees it.
Clara, it was so good I forgot it was mine.
Those long nights, lamp and candle. I got it down
almost the way I heard it. Just here and there
I think it needs a small touch of brown.

The Senator Explains a Vote

It's not my office, after all; it's yours.
I'm always pleased to see the folks I work for.
To tell the truth, I half expected you.
I know that you're unhappy; I read your letters.

You put me on the payroll to do a job
the way you want it done; and so I do,
when I can put a name to what you want.
Sometimes the public will's so faint a thing
it's hard to find it, then I use my own.

Some tell me that I've lost the common touch
and ought to be brought home and put to work.
The fact is, being here, things do look different.
You know how the slope of a straight road
climbing a hill way off ahead of you
may look like a perpendicular rise.
You have to get close to see it right.
But you can find metaphors enough
to say you see things better from a distance.

I'm digressing. Truth is, you credit me
for more effect on history than I have.
Once I thought the sounds of what I said
would last forever, give or take a year.
I also cared a lot what others said.
You start to think, though, as you get older,
what history books will say. That question has turned
some presidents and a few supreme court
judges into decent human beings.

That's something there we ought to think about,
what we elect, electing a human being.
We've known many a grief and many a grave
and now and then a happy half an hour,
but these have not told us very much
about what we are. Talking late,
we have sometimes confessed a fear of computers,
not wanting to say that we are computers, too,
for we are slow and move at our own behest.
On the other side we keep a distance
between ourselves and creatures. We rarely see this.
Gorillas make us nervous; even dogs do.
Between the sinless flesh and the sinless brain
we look uneasily in both directions
and hope for kind attention when we are dead.

It's hard to know, though, with what hard eyes
history may see us. We say to ourselves
that time will vindicate that one, or that one,
but who knows an hour ahead? All we can do
is make a few decisions and die with them.
History is going where it will.

But this is not what you want to know.

The fact is, the world is being invaded
and there is nothing we can do to stop it.
They will capture every government office,
they will control every church and school,
every position of power in the marketplace.
Everything we have will be theirs,
and there is no way for us to stop them
though every last one of us were Herod.
They are the children who were born last night.

While we browse through the evening paper
the streptococcus spawns generations,
but trees, if they could see us, would see us move
so fast we might be invisible.
We measure time by how much time we take.
Perhaps we should be still for a little while
and let things pass. But that isn't in us.

Anyway, if you can't cast a few
votes of your own, why come here at all,
a place full of people you don't like,
except to get your name in the almanac—
which, I may as well admit, is something.
My mother would have loved to see it there.

Why am I telling you this? I'm very sorry;
the bell you hear means I have a roll call.
Has anyone offered you coffee? Please keep the cups.
They have the insignia of the Senate on them.

In Extremis *in Hardy, Arkansas*

My client is a scoundrel and a thief,
the prosecutor says. While he was not
arrested for a scoundrel, I admit it.
Now he says he is a liar, too.
Using the language in the strictest sense
a rhetorician, yes, would say he lied,
but what he said he said in self-defense,
and after the fact, long after the fact.
I mean, when he was captured, he denied
he was a thief. But can a man be blamed
for letting the justice system do its job
without his crying, "Warm, cool, warm"?
The point is this: before no onerous act
did this man say, "Moth may corrupt, and rust,
but I will not break in." He never claimed
to be the sort of man that you could trust.
He lied not to get, but to get away.

If you are a Jew or a Muslim, you have to say
of course you want to take the eyes and teeth.
We know the hard laws of Abraham
our cousins live by, being out of grace.
But all of us have sinned and fallen short.

You must forgive me. That was out of place.
My head apologizes for my heart.
There are no pulpits in this country's courts
and that is meet and right. So mote it be.

A legend, then, for we can learn from legends:
People once believed a wound would get well
if one could have the blade that made the wound
be blest and polished and put to holy use;
and would, conversely, start to run and smell
if that blade were buried in corruption.
No soldier after battle cleaned his sword,
but stuck it in the dung of cows and pigs.
They might have used the cesspool of a prison
the prosecutor means to send this man to
and so ensure the festering of our wounds.
If you say, as I have watched you say,
my client is hopeless, lost among the lost,
you put yourselves in peril. That is despair.

God knows what made the sad man you see,
but I will not insult you with sentiment.
I may only say, to make a point,
how being scorned and scorning come together
like two ends of a tunnel. Go in at one,
sooner or later you come out at the other.

Patient friends, this man has fallen short.
If that were all that you were charged to know,
we could have gone home long ago.
The prosecutor, who had an easy task
compared to mine, the truth being with him,
has left no doubt of it, and little to ask
of you but mercy. All of us can see
my client is a scoundrel and a thief.
Ah, but my friends, you would let him go free
if you could know the man he meant to be.

After the Revolution for Jesus
a Secular Man Prepares His Final Remarks

What the blind lost when radio
gave way to TV,
what the deaf lost when movies
stopped spelling out words and spoke,
was a way back in. Always, this desire
to be inside again, when the doors are closed.

The thought of being disconnected
from history or place can empty the heart;
we are most afraid,
whatever else we fear,
of feeling the memory go, and of exile.
And death, which is both at once.

Still, as our lives
are the inhalations and exhalations of gods
we ought not fear those things we know will come
and ought not hope for what we know will not.
The dogs that waited for soldiers to come home
from Philippi, New Guinea, Pennsylvania,
are all dead now whether or not the men
came back to call them.

There is no constancy but a falling away
with only love as a temporary stay
and not much assurance of that.

The desert religions are founded on sandy ways
to set ourselves free from that endless tumbling downward.
Thus we endow ourselves with gods of purpose,
the purposes of gods, and do their battles.

We are sent to war for money, but we go for God.

Prison is no place for living
but for reliving lives.
I remember a quarrel of students
proving, reproving the world;
a woman taking love
she didn't want, but needed
like a drowning swimmer
thrown a strand of barbed wire
by a kind stranger standing on the shore.

Imperfect love in that imperfect world
seemed elegant and right.
Now the old air that shaped itself to our bodies
will take the forms of others.
They will laugh with this air and pass it through their bodies
but days like ours
they will not come again to this poor planet.

I am reinventing our days together.
A man should be careful with words
at a time like this,
but lies have some attraction over the truth;
there is something in deceitful words
that sounds good to the ear.

The first layer of paint conceals the actor;
the second conceals the paint.

By which sly truth we have come to where we are.

I can hear brief choirs of rifles.
Inside my head
naked women wander toward my bed.
How gently they lie there, loving themselves to sleep.

What do we know that matters that Aeschylus did not know?

I do believe in God, the Mother and Father,
Maker of possibility, distance, and dust,
who may never come to judge or quicken the dead
but does abide. We live out our lives
inside the body of God,
a heretic and breathing universe
that feeds on the falling of sparrows
and the crumbling of nations,
the rusting away of metal
and the rotting of wood.
I will be eaten by God.
There is nothing to fear.
To die, the singers believe, is to go home.
Where should I go, going home? Lord, I am here.

The Aging Actress Sees Herself
a Starlet on the Late Show

MONOLOGUE – X PERSONA POEM X (handwritten)

For centuries only painters, poets, and sculptors
had to live with what they did as children.
Those who trod the boards—I love that—
said their first stumbling lines into air.
Some do still, but most of us who are known
and loved for being people we are not
have reels and reels of old film unrolling
behind us nearly as far as we can remember.
We drag it everywhere. How would you like
your first time doing something to keep repeating
for everyone to look at all your life?

How would you like someone who used to be you
fifty years ago coming into this room?
How would you like it, never being able
to grow old all together, to have yourself
from different times of your life running around?

How would you like never being able
to stop moving, always to be somewhere
walking, crying, kissing, slamming a door?
You can feel it, millions of images moving;
no matter how small or disguised, you get tired.
How would you like never being able
completely, really, to die? I love that.

Ruby Tells All

When I was told, as Delta children were,
that crops don't grow unless you sweat at night,
I thought that it was my own sweat they meant.
I have never felt as important again
as on those early mornings, waking up,
my body slick, the moon full on the fields.
That was before air-conditioning.
Farm girls sleep cool now and wake up dry
but still the cotton overflows the fields.
We lose everything that's grand and foolish;
it all becomes something else. One by one,
butterflies turn into caterpillars
and we grow up, or more or less we do,
and, Lord, we do lie then. We lie so much
truth has a false ring and it's hard to tell.

I wouldn't take crap off anybody
if I just knew that I was getting crap
in time not to take it. I could have won
a small one now and then if I was smarter,
but I've poured coffee here too many years
for men who rolled in in Peterbilts,
and I have gotten into bed with some
if they could talk and seemed to be in pain.

I never asked for anything myself;
giving is more blessed and leaves you free.
There was a man, married and fond of whiskey.
Given the limitations of men, he loved me.
Lord, we laid concern upon our bodies
but then he left. Everything has its time.
We used to dance. He made me feel the way
a human wants to feel and fears to.
He was a slow man and didn't expect.
I would get off work and find him waiting.
We'd have a drink or two and kiss awhile.
Then a bird-loud morning late one April
we woke up naked. We had made a child.
She's grown up now and gone though God knows where.
She ought to write, for I do love her dearly
who raised her carefully and dressed her well.

Everything has its time. For thirty years
I never had a thought about time.
Now, turning through newspapers, I pause
to see if anyone who passed away
was younger than I am. If one was
I feel hollow for a little while
but then it passes. Nothing matters enough
to stay bent down about. You have to see
that some things matter slightly and some don't.
Dying matters a little. So does pain.
So does being old. Men do not.
Men live by negatives, like don't give up,
don't be a coward, don't call me a liar,
don't ever tell me don't. If I could live
two hundred years and had to be a man
I'd take my grave. What's a man but a match,
a little stick to start a fire with?

My daughter knows this, if she's alive.
What could I tell her now, to bring her close,
something she doesn't know, if we met somewhere?
Maybe that I think about her father,
maybe that my fingers hurt at night,
maybe that against appearances
there is love, constancy, and kindness,
that I have dresses I have never worn.

From *Living on the Surface*

The Book

I held it in my hands while he told the story.

He had found it in a fallen bunker,
a book for notes with all the pages blank.
He took it to keep for a sketchbook and diary.

He learned years later, when he showed the book
to an old bookbinder, who paled, and stepped back
a long step and told him what he held,
what he had laid the days of his life in.
It's bound, the binder said, in human skin.

I stood turning it over in my hands,
turning it in my head. Human skin.

What child did this skin fit? What man, what woman?
Dragged still full of its flesh from what dream?

Who took it off the meat? Some other one
who stayed alive by knowing how to do this?

I stared at the changing book and a horror grew,
I stared and a horror grew, which was, which is,
how beautiful it was until I knew.

He Glimpses a Nobler Vision
for Ed Asner

He worried every morning about the earth,
about the ozone layer wearing away,
about the suffocation of fish in the sea.
Then watching TV one day
he heard astronomers speak of uncountable planets,
apogee and perigee,
sun beyond cooling sun through unthinkable space,
with primal soup on some and civilization
burgeoning, maybe, on every millionth one.

So he said, Vanity, vanity,
something such as we are will scurry on,
it doesn't matter where.

He thought of something like people breathing air
or something like air, and of grace.
This brought him peace for a little while,
then, thinking too long, he thought

There might not be any elephants there.

And he was back again, with all he could bear.

Thinking about Bill, Dead of AIDS

We did not know the first thing about
how blood surrenders to even the smallest threat
when old allergies turn inside out,

the body rescinding all its normal orders
to all defenders of flesh, betraying the head,
pulling its guards back from all its borders.

Thinking of friends afraid to shake your hand,
we think of your hand shaking, your mouth set,
your eyes drained of any reprimand.

Loving, we kissed you, partly to persuade
both you and us, seeing what eyes had said,
that we were loving and were not afraid.

If we had had more, we would have given more.
As it was we stood next to your bed,
stopping, though, to set our smiles at the door.

Not because we were less sure at the last.
Only because, not knowing anything yet,
we didn't know what look would hurt you least.

The Man Who Stays Up Late

He knows that when he has to go to sleep
there will be people waiting there,
standing around with unattractive patience
ready to film the picture. Every night
they shoot the same scene: a hotel room,
neon blinking on the dirty windows.
Inside the room a tall and foreign woman
is standing silently in her underwear.
She nearly smiles. With long creeping fingers
she frees it of its tender obligations.
But then they have to shoot it over again,
over and over again, until at last
the sun swelling behind her wakes him up.

Before

Before word of his painting got around
Van Gogh spent a year in a coal mine
preaching the word of God underground
to miserable men. For dragging the divine
so close to hell the church kicked him out.
This is what his paintings were all about.

Conrad earned his first living afloat.
So did Samuel Clemens. When they got
themselves settled on dry land and wrote
all of those books, they were writing what
they'd learned when they were doing what they did.
For thirty years, Charles Bukowski hid

among the horseplayers where, fast word by word
and bet by bet, he managed to survive,
while he put into shape the world he heard,
as all of us must finally contrive
to hold on to anything we've won
by making what we do from what we've done.

Geoffrey Chaucer lived with Priest and Knight,
Prioress and Nun, Pardoner and Bitch;
he also lived as Franklin. Turning to write,
he wrote about them all. What we watch
or wallow in is all that we can share.
Anything else is dreamstuff. Is air.

We bury this, though, and we let the art
rise from those graves as if it came from air.
So it is with love. When we start
to touch and wallow, sweaty, slick, and bare,
we never mention where we learned the touch
that gives such pleasure. The fact is, we're such
incredible creatures we find it hard to say
to one another, "Someone hitherto
taught me what I'll teach you how to play;
I'll show you what one showed me how to do."
But who wants a priori? Who invents?
In loving, new is not worth two cents
no matter the myth. We find in dusty shops,
with always three globes above the door,
half-remembered faces, sweet shapes.
For every good there was a good before.
If now there is none but us, when we undress
bless them for when they sweated against us (yes).

Missing Persons

To judge by what they wore on weekdays,
he worked in, say, a factory near here;
she did what sort of thing a woman does

in matching blouse and slacks and flat heels.
Wait tables, probably, or fix hair.
They drove a pickup truck with ragged holes

where rust had eaten through, and a fender loose.
Monday through Friday at seven they rattled west.
At six they rattled home. In more or less

the time it took him to wash away the grease
they would come out again. The very worst
to say about them, across the ragged grass,

is they were beautiful. In tux and fur
they carefully uncovered a vintage Corvette, bone white,
and drove to the east. Saturday by four

they were like us again and the car was wrapped,
and they were off together to who knows what
in the old pickup truck with the seats ripped.

One day he drove the Corvette back alone,
covered it there and there he lets it sit.
He spends all weekend here and the small lawn

is growing into a wilderness of weeds.
Sometimes he hangs a gun above the seat
and heads the truck south, toward the woods.

So there you are. The only one remaining
out of two women and two men
is one silent, restless, redneck man.
But who's to say these facts have any meaning?

For Reuben, at Twelve Months

Whatever else you come to be
you will always be a year,
with numbers starting out from here
and going past where I can see,
if you are clever and cock an ear
for beast of old and boast of new,
if you are careful and keep an eye
peeled for the trolls of derring-do.
It took some luck to come this far.
That's half the game, to see how high
a number you can say you are.

The other half of you is who.
Take turns, be plain, settle for less
when less is fair, and be discreet.
Try not to waste anything.
Remember that everyone you meet
is a battlefield. If you never guess
what all the counting ought to bring
a being to, let it be done
for the harmless joy. If the world's a mess,
if we are all run into the ground,
it was good to count. The world you found
is all there is and better than none.
Sometimes it isn't bad at all,
this very like a floating ball
where marvels are many and you are one.

The Gift of Prophecy Lost

Late one Saturday morning I sat reading Hardy again
drinking a Bloody Mary in a cabin beside a lake
in the Missouri mountains while someone somewhere close
was playing country music. And then the print blurred.
The lyrics faded out. I blinked against a light
that filled the entire room till nothing cast a shadow
then went away as quickly. If this was spiritual
or physiological I had no way of knowing.
I only knew a sadness as if there had been something
to see in those few seconds that I had not seen.

An August Evening outside of Nashville

Seeing a chipmunk in the yard
holding a nut between its paws
while a jay in cold regard,
in a kind of punk repose,
sheds upon it what might be
contempt, for birds in Tennessee;

following a changing cloud
while my eyelids fill with lead;
hearing the wild bees grow loud
while a wobbling, overfed
goose scolds a lazy dog
and fungus on a rotting log

makes shapes I find a message in;
when a breeze takes the sweat
barely off my bare skin,
I can almost forget
how you were with dirty feet
all tangled in my sweaty sheet.

Rituals

I just got here myself and I feel like hell.
Yesterday I went and buried my brother.
Seven old friends helped me carry the casket
and then we went and got drunk together.
My brother killed himself. He took a dive
from ten stories up. He left his will
and wallet and pen and glasses, coins and keys,
neatly lined up on the window sill.
He didn't leave any kind of message.

OK. We begin with the mash. It's this stuff here;
it's nothing but corn and sugar, allowed to sit
for seven days or so. It's basically beer.
I didn't invent any part of this
but I have come to think I have a way
of making it go right, a kind of touch,
not going against the grain, you might say.

My brother was a preacher. He used to stand
in front of the altar rail wiping his brow,
calling, Won't you come? Won't you come?
calling, Come tonight, come now.
He used to put me in mind of a man I saw
in front of a strip joint. He'd wave and shout,
cracking the door to show a flash of flesh,
This is the place your mother warned you about.

I surely didn't invent this. Whoever did
was dead so long ago I doubt if years
had any numbers yet to know them by.
I took it as it was told. Now it's yours.
You have to pass it along or it doesn't work.

So. You have three canisters, called in turn
cooker and thumper—you see they sit over flame—
and then the flake. Real fire. You have to burn
some kind of gas to do this indoors.
Outdoors you burn anything you've got.
The cooker holds the mash, but not too much.
When the stuff gets sufficiently hot
it passes through the aforementioned thumper
into the aforementioned flake
whence it drips out a small spigot.
It breaks at the worm—the first drip is the break,
the spigot's the worm—at, say, sixty proof,
at a hundred seventy-five degrees or so,
then it shoots as high as two hundred.
The drops at first will come very slow
then slowly faster. You catch it in a beaker,
then you pour it into a mason jar.
The proof begins to fall very quickly.
Every half pint it drops as far
as ten proof a jar over the whole.
A spoon of moonshine over a match will do
to test the proof. It pops into flame.
You learn to read proof in the shades of blue.
Then you can say, Hell, as you sometimes will,
this ain't worth giving away, or you can say,
I'm going to ask some friends to come over.
A bad year deserves a good day.

Don't get lost going back. You won't see
the signs you had for markers coming out.
They're facing the wrong way. Watch for *Baitshop
and Christian Bookstore.* Then after just about
two miles turn right. A barn roof will say
See Rock City. Jesus Christ Is King.
Turn left two miles farther. A rock will say
An Isolated Virtue Is a Terrible Thing.

There's not a bait and bookshop anymore.
We use the sign to give directions by.
Something like the light of a dead star.
If you've never been here before
it's still one way of knowing where you are.

The Ghost of His Wife
Comes to Tell Him How It Is

Of course you're dreaming. That's how I got here.
How else do you expect to see and hear me?
Stop trying to wake yourself. Jesus Christ!
I met him, you know. He really pays attention
to all the new people. We aren't thought of
as people, though, exactly. They call us ghosts.
No kidding. Ghosts. We don't go to heaven
until we're easy being what we are.
I'm working on that. The big problem now
is learning not to pay attention to time.

The difference is, time changes nothing.
The hell is, I still feel it passing.

A minute passes for you, and you're a minute
closer to where you're going, finally death.
In death you're never closer to anything.

What the hell are you nodding about?
You don't know a thing about forever.
Forever is full of now. That's something else
I'm still trying to get used to.

Now, for you, is three generations
with yours in the middle, all populated
by people you can see. Farther away,
we get soft and hazy like someone
seen through a screen door at dusk.
Talking to children at breakfast or bedtime,
now is three minutes or three seconds.

For me, who is nothing, not even fog,
who is only awareness without form,
now is never. Try living with that.

That's not at all what I came about.
I came to say before the last sense
of who you are fades away like a smell
in the sweet evening air, that it's all right.
Do what you have to do. Don't think about me.

I could say I love you but I don't.
Love is more substantial than I am.
Still I cared enough to come and say this.
The care was all I was, and now it's gone.
And who are you? And what am I doing here?

The Journalist Buys a Pig Farm

I got tired of writing the wrong stories.
Not to say there weren't interesting stories,
but we have put our minds on trivial things,
events that interest us for what they are,
and not for what they mean—planes falling,
acts of terrorism, murders, elections,
any public suffering, public power.
These sit above the fold on the front page,
while countless other moments, barely noticed,
tell us everything we need to know.

Here in the second half of the twentieth century
in a small Delta town, on a doctor's desk,
I saw three thermometers labeled in turn
oral, rectal, colored. It's not to laugh.
Or who can say if it's to laugh or not.

Late in the fourth quarter, in a vacant lot
in a small mountain town with a courthouse
surrounded by blackjack and pin oak trees
across the highway from weedy tracks
I saw on one of those rusty marquees
that get towed about from place to place:
See in Wax the Lives of Christ and Elvis!

We always say a little more than we mean.

After the two-minute warning a judge in a case
involving dancers has ruled that only nipples
and not the rest of the breast are obscene.
To laugh or not, those were the real stories.

I'm going to go raise pigs now and read
biographies and listen to old music.

A long time I tried to deal with truth
as if a truth were true for everyone.
No. It's true for those who know it's true.

I call this a truth, for one example,
that given what we are and what we do
we have to think continually of heroes
or be dragged to madness of some sort
in which we are ones, as we have dreamed, and zeroes,
however serious and of good report.
If you can say that's not true, it's not.
It's so if you know it's so. Then you can see
how nigh impossible it finally got,
how head-down hard it did come to be
putting the world to words. I tell you what.

He Speaks to His Arguing Friends and to Himself

Rattle, rattle. There is no question
except the question of final cause.
The soul, free will, the afterlife,
the dream of universal laws,
prayer, and sacrifice, and honor,
works, and faith, and greed, and lust
might mean something or might not
depending on the source of dust.

Think of all there is as nothing,
not an atom, not a quark,
unexisting in a place,
pure unplace, not light, not dark.
Imagine that it all explodes
(although there's nothing to explode)
till matter and energy come to be.
This is one impossible road.

Imagine a mind that always was,
where In the beginning makes no sense.
Think it thinks us into being.
Think it knows us past our ends.
Given the mind, it came from where?
Or, free of it, we came from what?
These are the only ways to come.
Either way, you'd bet not.

But we have believed through such pain
and made such music for so long
that it would be a hurt and shame
if we should learn that we were wrong.
We have enough to fret about.
Almost all of us concur,
we'll live with the holidays we have
and the grace of God as if it were.

A Glass Darkly
for Will Campbell

At one of those bars where they weigh you at the door
so you don't fight out of your class
I took a stool away from the jukebox
and nodded toward a beer. I was slammed a glass.

The bartender looked like he'd sat on the bank all day
and still didn't have a full string.
You could look straight into his eyes
and see the back of his skull. "There's not a thing,"

I said to the man on my left, "gets cold as beer."
I asked him how he was doing. He gave me a look
to say his heart would last him the rest of his life.
"Homemade," he said, "is better." I guess it took

another two glasses to tell about
my mother, who doubted God. He gave me a glance
to say he didn't believe I told him that.
"Like all this," he said, "is stupid chance.

Ask about the planets and all the stars.
Ask about a snow goose, how it goes
to Alaska and back, not ever getting lost.
How about your finger fits your nose?

How about that woman?" You wouldn't believe
that woman waiting tables, whatever she said.
She wasn't a common truck-stop beauty.
Her smile smeared the air when she turned her head.

You could make love to her with one foot in a fire.
I stared at her with total disregard.
"That's a caramel-covered ball bearing,"
he said, to say that she was secretly hard.

"When people say ritual," I said,
"they intend graduation. They don't intend
paying bills or castrating hogs
or drinking in a bar at the back end

of a stingy day." The lady wiping up
said, "Do you want another?" He said, "No'm,
I better not." Still he didn't leave.
"Where are you from," I said. He said, "Home."

From *Adjusting to the Light*

Rodin: The Cathedral
On Coming upon It Unprepared

We had an hour. "—and on the way," she said,
"I want to show you something." A pair of hands
giving empty space a sacred shape,
sacred because a fool understands
a vaulted configuration closing upward.

If hands could dream, they might aspire to this,
to be tense and easy, in charge and groping,
wrapping around a holy nothing. Thus,
the mute might articulate a prayer
with these most human muscles, chosen bones,
by which we came, hand over hand, this far.

Through curving years I have been sustained by stones,
David, the Pietà. Now, two more hands.

"Are you all right?" she said. "We have to leave."

"It's strange," I said. "At first it made me happy
and then it made me sad." She said, "Like love?"

More than love, this trickery of light,
a frozen mathematics of the eye,
a wedding of love and logic we call art,
a dark we see and the light we see it by.

Beauty is in the marriage. Our delight
is in the prospect. The lagging sadness lies
in living to know that though it is made of us
we never can quite see what it signifies.

Adjusting to the Light

—air—air! I can barely breathe . . . aah!
Whatever it was, I think I shook it off.
Except my head hurts and I stink. Except
what is this place and what am I doing here?

Brother, you're in a tomb. You were dead four days.
Jesus came and made you alive again.

Lazarus, listen, we have things to tell you.
We killed the sheep you meant to take to market.
We couldn't keep the old dog, either.
He minded you. The rest of us he barked at.
Rebecca, who cried two days, has given her hand
to the sandalmaker's son. Please understand
we didn't know that Jesus could do this.

We're glad you're back. But give us time to think.
Imagine our surprise to have you—well,
not well, but weller. I'm sorry, but you do stink.
Everyone, give us some air. We want to say
we're sorry for all of that. And one thing more.
We threw away the lyre. But listen, we'll pay
whatever the sheep was worth. The dog, too.
And put your room the way it was before.

During a Funeral Service
the Mind of the Young Preacher
Wanders Again

"We come," he says, "to bury an empty shell."
Which is true and says nothing. He thinks of this.
He thinks of Hume. So far as he can tell
nobody sees the small parenthesis

enclosing his head, although the old phrases
which are his obligation continue to pour
out of his mouth. He lifts his eyes and gazes
past the congregation, past the shore

on which, he tells them, all the believing dead
are waiting for us always. He shuts his eyes.
He is unaccountably tired. He bows his head,
in which a thought is worming its way. He tries

to concentrate on saying what ought to be said
to people undone as one from this man,
that he is not gone for good, but gone ahead.
It's happened before. He does the best he can,

though at times like this—it is a growing peace—
he half suspects the dead don't ever look
our way again, once gone from this blue space,
don't have the wherewithal for looking back,
and have no truck, if he knows the simple truth,
with any trick we fall for, not life, not death.

A Day in the Death

He is amazed how hard it is to die.
He lies in the hospital bed, his shallow breaths
audible in the hall. He wonders why—
and tries to laugh because he knows—the deaths
of heroes always seem to be so quick.
Because, he knows, heroes have to fight,
and die fighting; also they rarely get sick.
A nurse looks into the room to say good night.
They don't tell each other what they know,
that both hope these words are the last he'll hear,
but guess they aren't. He thinks of the undertow
all swimmers swimming in strange waters fear,
that grabs you from below. He tries to sink
deep enough beneath the surface of sleep
to be found there and lost. There is a stink
thickening in the room. He knows the cheap
perfume Death wears. Why does she stand around?
Why doesn't the bitch take him? He tries to laugh
and this time does, and jerks at the new sound.
Well, half is already gone; the other half
could be a survivor of Buchenwald. Today
a counselor held his hand and told him again
to let go, to let it slip away.
He turned back to see how long it had been
since he had held on. He almost said,
"I'm trying. Something's stuck. Give me a shove."
He almost did. He squeezed the hand instead,
once for reasons forgotten and once for love.
But now he tries to sleep, pretends he is led
down through a wandering tunnel, sweetly gray,
to join the deep society of the dead,
afraid when the sun comes they'll send him away,
back to that room, back to that shrinking bed,
to lie there, being a lie, another day,
his eyes, his enormous eyes, eating his head.

On Not Writing a Love Poem

How do I say
what everybody says
as if it hasn't been said
by everyone?

What can I do
(considering all the dead)
that isn't banal, pretending
it hasn't been done?

There is no death,
love, birth, that isn't trite.
If all our passions are long-
discovered islands

patterned with footprints,
a Sunday tourist sight,
let people (cupping their ears)
say, "Listen: what silence."

Excuse Me

Give me just a second before you start.
Let's agree on what you're reading here.
Let's call it a poem, a poem being an act
of language meant to hold its own exceptions,
which you therefore read with a double mind,
accepting and rejecting what you find.

If part of what you find is what you brought,
let's call this reading a poem, one of the games
imaginations play when they meet.
If you suspect you may not have the wit
to face the other player, one on one,
then you can be a deconstructionist
and make believe the other doesn't exist,
though that will be like sitting on one end
of a seesaw in summer, wishing you had a friend.

To a Friend, an Unhappy Poet

You fret how few now read what's hard to write.
There barely are any
but this is not something we can fix.
There never were many.

About the same percentage of people always
could love a noun.
What mother in London's slums opened her Blake
or Milton after the children were yelled down?

More to the point, how many quoting stocks
could quote Carew?
How many people in Mansfield Park read Austen?
The question was never how many but why and who.

Because millions can say the printed word
you think they should read
not signs and menus and scores and labels but us.
They know what they need.

The Death of Chet Baker

Somewhere between *Amazing Grace*
and *Great Balls of Fire* we heard
the horn first and then the voice
like Billie Holiday's. Old Bird,

he knew a secret. So did Diz.
But Chet, he struck him up a deal
with dark angels. Angel he was
and dark he was. Truth to tell,

he darkened till he fell away
wearing twice his fitting years,
still playing at what he had to say,
sometimes putting on some airs

but they were his. He put them on
like pants and shoes, a wrinkled shirt.
What do we feel, now that he's gone?
What of the hollow? How does it hurt?

Hotly as shame? Sharply as scorn?
As dimly as an old rebuke?
There was a hophead with a horn
who stopped a concert to puke,

who couldn't read the notes he played,
who couldn't love a person long,
who blew the breath of souls afraid
into muted, seamless song.

But what to pity these pitiless days?
He had his dreams and methadone,
we have tapes and CDs,
Time after Time, When Your Lover Has Gone.

CDs do what was done before
over and over and over and over,
never adding a note more
if we should listen to them forever.

Wherever we are he isn't there.
Love him. Love him in the loss
for all the things he did with air.
The thrill is gone. Poor Chet. Poor us.

    Epitaph
Once a jazzman, playing high,
raised up his horn and tried to fly.
He got above the oxygen
and fell back to earth again.
The body here beneath this stone
was Chet Baker, who has flown.

Things

J.C., 1916–1986

The day we went to visit the house of the poet
I sat in the chair he sat in when he died
to look at the last things he looked at:
the cribbage board; the blue wall; the clock,
the slow brass pendulum; the deck of cards;
the small Picasso, slapdash black on white,
almost oriental, one foot by two;
the black round telephone with the circular dial;
the rug with wine roses; books on the floor.
I sat until the pendulum took my attention
to feel what he might have felt, sitting there.

For nothing, of course, for all my foolishness.
The dying gave the room its brown meaning.
When he sat down, the chair was just a chair.

During the Hymn before the Christmas Sermon the Mind of the Young Preacher Wanders Again

For God to send a son into the world
meant, in fact, for Him to give His son
into the realm of time. But how could the two
speak with each other, then? Thy will be done,

orders, supplications, the sound waves
built on passing time, though it doesn't pass
inside the mind of God. He must hear nothing,
at rest in an infinite never. An always. I guess.

What do I know about space and time?
Almost nothing. I ought to hide my face,
sitting here hoping to know God,
whose simplest thought may be time and space.

But how would He think, time being nothing to Him?
There's a puzzle for you. I would think thought
means process of a sort, and process, time,
though I have only the math that I was taught.

The fact is we have little enough to work with
in coming to see what might make any sense
inside the mind, whatever it is, of God.
What we call acts and scientists call events
are equally beyond us. We are like fruit
hungering to understand the tree.
(He likes it but he doesn't have the time
to lean back and enjoy the simile.

The closing chords have moved him to his feet.
The people sit and wait. He looks at them
so long they start to look at one another.)
"In Judea," he says, "in Bethlehem . . ."

The Art Photographer Puts His Model at Ease — DRAMATIC MONOLOGUE —

IAMBIC PENTAMETER

Well, good. You got here. Let me take your things.
I hope it wasn't hard to find your way.
Have a seat by the window. A new model,
I like to talk awhile and get to know her.   BLANK VERSE
It lets us relax. I do mean both of us.
Truth to tell, I'm a shy person myself.
I know that's something I have to get around.

I hope you remembered about the underwear.
The lines from all the elastic and the straps
can take an hour or two to go away.
You're on the clock from when we close the door.
I can't pay you to sit around and wait
for bra and panty impressions to smooth out.
It's just a practical thing, you understand.

But it's all right. There isn't any hurry.
A couple of minutes now, relaxing a little,
it's going to save me more than what it costs me,
once we go inside and get to work.

I know you feel nervous, not wearing any.
Well, but that's not quite the problem is it?
More my knowing you don't have any on.
You'll get used to that. After a while
you won't even think about it. I certainly don't.
I hate to see that happen, to tell the truth.
There's something about a model the first time,
something—what can I call it? Modesty, maybe?—
that says you're not used to being looked at.
There's a sweetness in such an innocence,
and I might say a sadness, that gets lost later.

So how do you pout? Let me see you pout.
Pretend that you're about to say *please,*
just with the last sniffle after you've cried.
How would you like a little glass of wine?
Sometimes it helps. It brings a light to the face.

I guess you're nervous now about getting undressed.
You don't have to do it in front of me.
You get behind a screen. There's a camisole there,
so you don't come out with nothing on.
Models don't walk around with nothing on.
The naked body walking around is erotic.
We have to be careful about that.
It's a very close relationship, artist and model.
I could tell you some that were great lovers.
And hell, no wonder.

Let me pour you some wine.
You'll find the studio chilly. I keep it that way.
It tightens the skin and brings the nipples out.
Look at the time. Where did the time go?
Go on and finish your wine. We want to be sure
you're feeling at ease in every part of your body.
I can't work with a self-conscious model.
If you're embarrassed others will be embarrassed.

I can tell you hadn't thought of that,
about how many people are going to see you.
You're also going to make a little money.

You truly are a very lovely woman.

Now sit up straight and hold your shoulders back.
Your breasts are set high and they hold to the center.
That's good. It means that when you lie down
they won't slide off your chest like fried eggs.

Now when we get inside, forget I'm here.
Get undressed and walk straight to the couch.
Breathe deeply. Let the camisole float to the floor.
Pretend you're waiting naked for a lover.
All art is pretend. You just forget I'm here.
If you can't do that, why don't you make believe
I'm watching you from a window across the street.
You just sit and think about your lover.
Then lie down. OK. I think we're ready.

[handwritten annotations: "MEANS TO BE DOING vs. REALITY OF WORDS", "EROTICISM - we were trying to avoid", "to go"]

179

Morning at the Zagorsk Monastery
outside Moscow

She bent so low
she bruised her gnarly knuckles against the ground.
She was so slow
she could barely keep even with her cane.
She was so old
she may not have remembered having teeth.
When she was told
the monastery was closed for the weekend
she was so sad
her tiny face screwed itself together.
She lived, she said
through the revolution, the civil war,
the stormblast
when Germany laid siege to Leningrad.
She meant to last
a few more years, so she could go to heaven
when everyone went,
with the last sunset of the second thousand years.
The last event.
That way she wouldn't have to go alone.
They said, she said,
we did not need to come here anymore,
Christ being dead,
killed in our streets in 1917.
What does that say?
Everybody we'll see in heaven is dead.
One blinding day
we'll all go up before Him, begging grace.
I am so old,
she said, that children cannot count that far.
I've never told
anybody all the things I know.
I say a prayer
for poor Joseph Stalin, for all those years
when he was there
in every mirror, in every telephone.

He comes in dreams,
bloody and torn, dripping with remorse,
or so it seems.
Who knows what is actual on this earth?
Nevertheless,
what it comes to, poor God being dead,
is saying yes.
That is what I say. It's what I've said
these awful years.
I don't see any point at all now
in spending tears
on those that haven't said it. Let them lie.
I almost grieved
once for old Stalin, who I suppose
truly believed
there wasn't any God, and now he knows.

Architecture of the American Mind

It happened, halfway through the nineteen hundreds,
that all things old and ugly were abhorrent.
The past, like unwanted knowledge, embarrassed people.
Buildings of red clay bricks on town squares
all over the country were given aluminum skin.

"We have a past," we said, "in our own way.
You'll see no sign of it here, look as you may."

During the century's closing years, the past,
working out from cornices and cracks,
was loved again, and many dollars were spent
to pull the skins away from the warm bricks.
Nobody recalled the strange embarrassment.

"We have a past," we said, "a yesterday
long, drab, and odd. Like London, you might say."

The Six Moral Virtues:
Grace, Style, Class, Humility, Kindness, and Wisdom

Not to glance at anyone else, looking full in the face
at someone telling a story a third time—this is grace.

Letting the crabby driver hold his hand a long while
before you drip a small tip coin by coin—this is style.

Ignoring knowing eyes, the grin behind the lifted glass,
as if there were no secrets to be known—this is class.

To die with everyone you know let loose from promises
with no small cry to call them after you, faint SOS,

but going in a style for those you leave to fumble toward
when you won't know, is style with class and grace, a closing chord.

I think if we had stopped to point them out, to say, You show
these somethings, What do you call them? You would have said,
    I don't know.

That's four of six. If you were somewhat kind, a little wise . . .
Here you would have said, now don't go getting into lies.

But I was there and am a witness here and I can swear
you carried them as quietly as the virus, and as unaware.

Pulling Back

Here in my drive in the rain,
a bright, little sprinkle of rain,
with the wipers turned off, I can see
a Monet of my house and my lawn,
and I wonder why anyone cares
what a newspaper editor thinks,
if a hippo is kin to a bear
or if one day the sun will burn out
or what seven-year-olds want to wear.

When I Am Dead, My Dearest

Sing what you want to sing. Theologize.
Let anyone who wants to lie tell lies.
What will I care, back in the past tense
with no ambition and not a gram of sense,
back where I was before a fear and a wish
joined to form a sort of finless fish
that learned to walk and have lips and smile?
I will go there to wait an endless while,
and neither think that wrong nor wish it right,
more than a rock in darkness hopes for light.
You will say my name, but less with years,
the children less than you and more than theirs.
It's mostly in our names, as they fray and thin,
blown on the breaths of aging friends and kin,
that in some tugging moments we may seem
to sleep on a little past the dream.

Coping

So let us suppose that after everybody
goes to bed or shift-work Monday night,
filled with sweet contingencies and regrets,
they wake or go home astonished at Wednesday morning.
Some might call in their debts, some pay their debts.
Others might argue whether a missing day
meant one day more or one day less to live.
Some would knock with warnings, door to door.
Some would do what they had planned for Tuesday
and never think about it anymore.

Hello. I'll Bet You Don't Know Who This Is.

A friend has come by after twenty years
and I am older than before he came.
The nervous socialist no longer stirs
behind the rimless glasses. Besides his name,

the voice, the glasses, hardly anything
is what he was. Can it have been so long?
He sits with his wife as we trade remembering
and looks at me as if I remember wrong.

Despairing of Understanding
We Fall into Decadence

Though all our innocence cannot console us
for what we don't know, sometimes even so,
there's pleasure in it. Full of ignorance

we lie on the living room rug empty as lizards.
By waning dinner candles and two small lamps
we kiss and read all night, Wyatt and Welty,

and others who taught us the world, who taught us time,
and change, the always faster breathing of time,
and the flickering possibilities of words.

Along its cold descent of days and nights
the tumbling earth turns us toward the sun
to send us to bed. Fumbling and out of phase

with the first stirring birds and yawning beasts
and countless imperceptibly shifting leaves,
we rouse ourselves past noon, with no chores done.

ICU: Space/Time in the Waiting Room

There faded from her features what was her.
She could have been her sister. A day or two,
she could have been a cousin. A couple more,
she might have been someone I never knew.

She was so far off and set on going,
I couldn't make her hear me yesterday.
She got smaller and smaller. Now this morning,
I think she could be coming back this way.

I Can Only Stay for Fifteen Minutes

"Oh," the doctor mumbled, "she's doing as well
as anyone could expect." He's said it before.
Still you lie here shrinking, cell by cell,
as if you don't understand what a deathbed's for.

If there is someone there at last to tell,
say that we want out easier. Say that we fear,
more than the face of God or faces of hell,
dying before we die. Say we'd prefer

not spending nine more months finding our way
back out of the world. The mind knows well enough.
It's this mule of a body that wants to stay,
forgetting and fussing till everything falls off.

The old gods might listen. They used to play
with all the fine distinctions: dignity, shame,
hubris, cowardice, watching night and day.
If they are out there still, they might still dream

of getting involved again. Tell them you came
one of the hard ways and how we can miss
deciding things for ourselves. Give them my name,
who comes up next and doesn't need any of this—
the little smell, the patience, the awful blame.

Closing the House

That's never going to fit inside the box.
They took the picture to help them do her hair.
I guess we just throw out the underwear
but what are we to do with all the books?
Praise Him, honey, she's gone to where He's at.
Love goes to love for all the love we miss.
Who can tell me what to do with this?
I think Aunt Agnes always wanted that.

Walking after Supper
for Howard Nemerov

It is when I have thought of the universe
expanding until an atom becomes the size
of a solar system and millions of years pass
during the forming of a single thought,
of some place where gigantic young are taught
that we were here (though this will be known
by no evidence but logic alone,
all signs of us, and even our sun, gone),
that I have sometimes had to remind myself
that, say, if in a car at a crosswalk
a woman waves for me to go ahead,
this act deserves attention; that her doing that
equals in gravity all that has ever been
or will have been when we and the sun are dead.
All this I think in Fayetteville, Arkansas,
frozen here on the curb, in love, in awe.

The Groom Kisses the Bride
and the Mind of the Young Preacher
Wanders Again

He knows what it signifies, lifting the veil,
but wonders where it started—the Gauls, the Huns;
maybe, he thinks, the Druids. Likely the Druids.
Say a thousand years, and the smelly beginnings.
Back to the shaman, singing the words of wedding
from Old High German *wager,* Old Norse *pledge.*
Back to the husband, Old Frisian, *house,* and *bondage.*
Back to the wife, of unknown origin.
Back to the circle of elders, closing and watching,
back to the careful lifting of the dress,
down to the bearskin rug, the body surprised,
until the lute signals the celebration
meaning another member of the tribe
might have been begun. How would that be,
he wonders, being one of such a circle,
unmoving, unmoved as the gray circling stones.
Or would they applaud? Why would they not applaud?

The laughing music from *Lohengrin* takes her away.
They will be children, he thinks, for a little while,
flesh upon flesh on the bed or the front room floor,
then they may learn to listen to slower songs.
Naked she would speak of the glory of God
". . . and God be with you always, go in peace,"
but everyone is gone, the organist, even,
has folded up her music and gone home.

Learning Russian

First the elaborate letters, then their sounds,
the fat, embarrassed tongue feeling its way,
and then the words, heavy with consonants,
tied uselessly together for something to say
to him that meets me mornings in the mirror,
both of us dour, both of us Muscovites:
I want to buy four refrigerators.

Learning the long winter, the snow-blue lights.
Then getting used to leaving small words out:
My mother old; I go work, good-bye.

Becoming romantic, the hand against the brow,
and then learning to build the occasional lie
I've learned to live with in my own language.
They work as well; we are what we are.

Then talking about the government in whispers,
loving the Winter Palace, hating the czar.

Mise-en-Scène

So his friends will think him smart
he grabs a chance to use words like *athwart,*
durst, epistaxis, dour, and *thence.*
He turns them lightly, given half a chance.

Chances are few, but now and then
he seems the most erudite of men.
Or so he thinks. Friends, I'm afraid,
think him gauche and largely gasconade.

On Seeing a Photograph by Matthew Brady

In 1863 whole towns
carried lunches to hillsides
to watch a war. Some made bets.
Some tried to recognize their kin.
Now my wife and I take meals
watching several worlds away
a war too big for battlefields,
a war too far for us to say
which are kin. All could as well
be kin for all that we can tell.

Out of a Clear Sky

You've wanted to hear my voice, so hear me now.
I know it must have seemed a long time.
You have to know I've carried you as a thought.
You're every one my creatures and I love you,
going about your wars and ball games.

You think I don't give my attention to games?
There is nothing, you might say, beneath me.
Though seen in another way, everything is.

Everything between us is paradox.
You've said you want to be the way I want you.
I have wanted to be whatever you wanted
whenever you called my name, whatever it was.
For some, a face with brief and human emotions.
For some, only a love that knows its name.
My name is, well, the cause of everything.

Some ask, If I created space and time,
where did I exist before I did it?
None of this is your concern at all.
All you have to know is, I am here.

Recall the lonely feeling when you doubt me.
Though when this occurs it's mostly my fault.
I could have had you smarter than you are.
Still, may I be praised, you are my thoughts.
I called it good. I still call it good.

I'm talking here. Is anybody listening?
Why aren't you on the rooftops, into the streets?
What do you think you're hearing here, thunder?
I'm not asking that to get an answer.
You know I know the answer before I ask.
It's just a way of moving a question forward,
like "Where is your brother?" Like "Who said you were naked?"
Like "How would you like to see the world on fire?"

That's just to scare you. I still hold the thought
wrapped in the thought I had of everything
flying away from me, with little clots
collecting here and there and having thoughts.

You are the sweetest, most chaotic thought
of all these thoughts that fly forth, making time.
I'll hold it till it all comes back to me.

And in the meantime, listen when I talk.
Why do you think I thought you in the beginning?

Folding His USA Today
He Makes His Point in the Blue Star Café

There's this bird I saw in the paper, they said
was a long time on that endangered list
but isn't now because they're all dead.
It didn't have a place to put its nest.
So what we're out is, we're out a bird.
It never weighed an ounce, and what I read,
the thing was hardly seen or even heard
by much of anyone. So now it's spread
across a half a page. Do-gooders, they'll
undo us yet. If it was, say, a deer,
that did some good. Or bass. OK. Or quail.
We are talking about a sparrow here.
Maybe there's something I don't understand.
Anyone's cooked a sparrow, raise your hand.

The Stripper

You're too young for this. I was twenty.
What are you? Eighteen, maybe? Seventeen?
You know the cops are going to check your papers.
What do they call you? Jean? They call you Jean?
That won't do. That won't do at all.
We'll need to find something sort of, well,
you know, a name nobody ever had.

You sure you want to do this? I wouldn't tell
no one I know to work here, a hundred men
yelling things to you about your tits,
you don't really feel complimented.
If I had a place to go, I'd call it quits
so quick you could put your hand in the hole
where I used to be. But when you're down,
I don't know; it makes you feel good
to be admired by a man from some town
where no one ever saw a woman naked
with all the lights turned on, married or not.

I assume Jean is your real name.
So keep it. I was told to teach you how
to move about and take your clothes off.
I guess you figure you can do that now,
except for being so bashful you can't talk.
Well, you don't have to talk. Just be sincere.
That's the whole secret, so everyone
can make believe that no one else is here.
Lord, look at you, honey. I bet you've got
half a Greyhound ticket still in your purse.

Pretty soon you won't know yourself
You won't even want to. What's worse,
not many others are going to know you, either.
Not men, I mean. Not in a happy way.
Every man wants his woman a secret.
Except in swimming. Swimming, the bitch can lay
her body down where everybody sees,
with nothing but her crotch and nipples hid.
You can't do that for cash and be a lady.
Though Gypsy Rose Lee was and did.
Once in a while somebody beats the odds.

I'm supposed to show you how to hunch.
The first thing is, not to be so fearful.
Shake it up a little. That buys your lunch.
It won't be you up here. You'll be a hundred
nights that used to be or might have been.

And smile at all the women. Some are here
to see what you have to show them, same as the men.

So, anyway. You got to have your props.
I use a chaste lounge and a telephone.
Use a wooden horse if you want to.
The only thing, you got to be alone.
Don't share the stage with anybody ever.
Scores every night are going to climb up here
in their imaginations. That's crowd enough.

You have to throw out a souvenir,
something cheap that you can buy a box of.
First they'll have the comic out there
relaxing everybody except you.
You'll be back there wondering what to wear.

You know they've brought you in to put me out.
I kind of thought they might be going to.
What can you do? You give them all you've got.
I don't know. I guess I take a few
too many now and then. I got some veins
you don't have to look too close to see.
It seems like every day I hang looser.
I look in the mirror, I can't believe it's me.

Anyway, start out with what you're wearing.
Button up your blouse all the way.
You have to begin with everything proper.
You'll probably end up wearing a negligee
that you can see through, but first of all,
you come in from a date. You close the door.
You pick his picture up and look at it.
You let your blouse and skirt fall to the floor.
Then your slip. You have to have a slip.
And then your bra first and then your pants.
Keep your stockings on. Real stockings.
Move slow. Slow to music. Like a dance.

You're pretty as anything I ever saw.
Let me ask you something. What would you do
if one of your family wandered in here?
Your daddy, say, but didn't know it was you.

There's this little place where I like to go.
They have good boiled shrimp and a nice bar.
We've done enough for now. I'd like to know
what magazines you read, if you like to sew,
and exactly who in the hell you think you are.

The Shrinking Lonesome Sestina

Somewhere in everyone's head something points toward home,
a dashboard's floating compass, turning all the time
to keep from turning. It doesn't matter how we come
to be wherever we are, someplace where nothing goes
the way it went once, where nothing holds fast
to where it belongs, or what you've risen or fallen to.

What the bubble always points to,
whether we notice it or not, is home.
It may be true that if you move fast
everything fades away, that given time
and noise enough, every memory goes
into the blackness, and if new ones come—

small, mole-like memories that come
to live in the furry dark—they, too,
curl up and die. But Carol goes
to high school now. John works at home
what days he can to spend some time
with Sue and the kids. He drives too fast.

Ellen won't eat her breakfast.
Your sister was going to come
but didn't have the time.
Some mornings at one or two
or three I want you home
a lot, but then it goes.

It all goes.
Hold on fast
to thoughts of home
when they come.
They're going to
less with time.

Time
goes
too
fast.
Come
home.

Forgive me that. One time it wasn't fast.
A myth goes that when the quick years come
then you will, too. Me, I'll still be home.

She Prays for Her Husband, the Good Pastor, Lying on His Deathbed at Last

He wants to go somewhere he hasn't been.
He's tired of where he's been. He wants to go
away from here, away from earth, from dirt.
He's tired of everything that humans know.
He longs to know what no one ever knew:
invisible shapes, a love without a name,
women and men who go about their being
without praise, ambivalence, or blame.
Hormones and hope and five-dollar perfume
take us places he has not been to much,
make us tell old lies to one another,
bore each other to sleep, and darkly touch.

Letters to newspapers, and bad sermons,
these were his major sins, his joy these.
Take his soul home and make it feel at home,
filled with the love of you and ill at ease.

The Serial Murderer Says Something to the Priest

If we all go, seeing we all were made
from nothing, to nothing again, I'm ready to go.
But if there is a place for beings to be
after we thought we had it out of the way,
someplace I might be met by shade after shade
of them that died in my hands, well, I confess,
that I would be uneasy. I'd be afraid.
But then I guess I'd naturally go to hell
and they'd be elsewhere, mostly. Truth to tell,
I'd rather be damned alone than have them wait,
watching for me to come to where they are,
hovering, silent, dark with knowledge and hate.
Still I'd rather face them again than forget
their grand, identical eyes, begging and wet.

Hello

Whoever you are, you have the number you dialed.
We probably could but will not come to the phone.
We can talk on the other side of the tone
unless you're the woman who stands every day
collecting columns of signatures in the mall,
the man we've been avoiding for weeks, the child
that rolled away and will not leave us alone.
If, on the other hand, this is a call
to tell us that you love us, give us a way
to be in touch again, the name of the bar,
maybe a number scribbled there on the wall,
the intersection nearest to where you are.
We've waited to hear you love us. It might not hurt
to know how much, but you don't have to say.
We probably couldn't handle it, anyway.
But bless your heart. Bless your heavy heart.

A Question of Time

"Have you ever done this with another man?"
He liked to ask me that at random moments,
in little cafés, once on a Ferris wheel.
I don't know why, a kind of game, I guess,
a way of being told what he had to hear.

I'd carried the word around for twelve years.
I was surprised to feel it coming out.
It should have lain there like the other times
but something in the question knocked it loose
and I was tired. We both should have been asleep.

I heard it coming as soon as I heard the question,
past my heart, through my throat, "Yes."
I felt a hollow place where the word had been.

He said, "I mean, since we've been married."
He couldn't let it go. I said, "Yes."
He looked from the sides of his eyes and saw I meant it.

He won't come back. I'd never ask him to.
First he was obsessed with the foolish question,
now he's obsessed with the answer. Still, I miss him.
I also miss the other man sometimes,
though I doubt that he could recall my name.

I let him do it because it made me feel good
to have somebody think that way about me.
It had nothing at all to do with him.

I got what I deserved. I did wrong.
But it was over so quickly, and it's been so long.

The Curator

We thought it would come, we thought the Germans would come,
were almost certain they would. I was thirty-two,
the youngest assistant curator in the country.
I had some good ideas in those days.

Well, what we did was this. We had boxes
precisely built to every size of canvas.
We put the boxes in the basement and waited.

When word came that the Germans were coming in,
we got each painting put in the proper box
and out of Leningrad in less than a week.
They were stored somewhere in southern Russia.

But what we did, you see, besides the boxes
waiting in the basement, which was fine,
a grand idea, you'll agree, and it saved the art—
but what we did was leave the frames hanging,
so after the war it would be a simple thing
to put the paintings back where they belonged.

Nothing will seem surprised or sad again
compared to those imperious, vacant frames.

Well, the staff stayed on to clean the rubble
after the daily bombardments. We didn't dream—
You know it lasted nine hundred days.
Much of the roof was lost and snow would lie
sometimes a foot deep on this very floor,
but the walls stood firm and hardly a frame fell.

Here is the story, now, that I want to tell you.
Early one day, a dark December morning,
we came on three young soldiers waiting outside,
pacing and swinging their arms against the cold.
They told us this: in three homes far from here
all dreamed of one day coming to Leningrad
to see the Hermitage, as they supposed
every Soviet citizen dreamed of doing.
Now they had been sent to defend the city,
a turn of fortune the three could hardly believe.

I had to tell them there was nothing to see
but hundreds and hundreds of frames where the paintings had
    hung.

"Please, sir," one of them said, "let us see them."

And so we did. It didn't seem any stranger
than all of us being here in the first place,
inside such a building, strolling in snow.

We led them around most of the major rooms,
what they could take the time for, wall by wall.
Now and then we stopped and tried to tell them
part of what they would see if they saw the paintings.
I told them how those colors would come together,
described a brushstroke here, a dollop there,
mentioned a model and why she seemed to pout
and why this painter got the roses wrong.

The next day a dozen waited for us,
then thirty or more, gathered in twos and threes.
Each of us took a group in a different direction:
Castagno, Caravaggio, Brueghel, Cézanne, Matisse,
Orozco, Manet, da Vinci, Goya, Vermeer,
Picasso, Uccello, your Whistler, Wood, and Gropper.
We pointed to more details about the paintings,
I venture to say, than if we had had them there,
some unexpected use of line or light,
balance or movement, facing the cluster of faces
the same way we'd done it every morning
before the war, but then we didn't pay
so much attention to what we talked about.
People could see for themselves. As a matter of fact
we'd sometimes said our lines as if they were learned
out of a book, with hardly a look at the paintings.

But now the guide and the listeners paid attention
to everything—the simple differences
between the first and post-impressionists,
romantic and heroic, shade and shadow.

Maybe this was a way to forget the war
a little while. Maybe more than that.
Whatever it was, the people continued to come.
It came to be called The Unseen Collection.

Here. Here is the story I want to tell you.

Slowly, blind people began to come.
A few at first then more of them every morning,
some led and some alone, some swaying a little.
They leaned and listened hard, they screwed their faces,
they seemed to shift their eyes, those that had them,
to see better what was being said.
And a cock of the head. My God, they paid attention.

After the siege was lifted and the Germans left
and the roof was fixed and the paintings were in their places,
the blind never came again. Not like before.
This seems strange, but what I think it was,
they couldn't see the paintings anymore.
They could still have listened, but the lectures became
a little matter-of-fact. What can I say?
Confluences come when they will and they go away.

From *Points of Departure*

Going Deaf

No matter how she tilts her head to hear
she sees the irritation in their eyes.
She knows how they can read a small rejection,
a little judgment, in every *What did you say?*
So now she doesn't say *What?* or *Come again?*
She lets the syllables settle, hoping they form
some sort of shape that she might recognize.
When they don't, she smiles with everyone else,
and then whoever was talking turns to her
and says, "Break wooden coffee, don't you know?"
She puts all she can focus into the face
to know if she ought to nod or shake her head.
In that long space her brain talks to itself.
The person may turn away as an act of mercy,
leaving her there in a room full of understanding
with nothing to cover her, neither sound nor silence.

How We May by Chance Pronounce
the Unsuspected Residence of a Ghost

I lifted a glass to get the waiter's attention.
"I'll be there directly," she said
across two tables.
One shade-spattered moment there was a backyard,
a woman in what we used to call a wash dress
calling from the kitchen,
with one elbow holding the screen door open,
drying her hands.

At the Children's Hospital in Little Rock

Scorning the schemes of nature,
by accident, illness, and murder,
chance hands the past our future
and ruins us out of order.

We hope and beg as we can,
tugging the hem of frost
as if we were children again.
Us first. Let us be first.

How Did You Ever Live without It?
A Peppermill with a Light!

How, indeed? For some do die without it.

The couple out of gas on the wrong county road,
the gray-skinned woman sleeping on the grate,
the miner, trapped and trying to lie still—
who heard from each of them the hopeless prayer
for someone to come in time with a peppermill?

But now a climber, lost on a steepening slope,
sees a dog pawing heavily toward him,
bellowing hope across the blue drifts.
The dog stands above him, panting white pillows.
The man squints to believe. The wood looks right.
He puts forth a hand, the freezing fingers
nearly afraid to close on the polished oak.
"Thank God, thank God," he says, seeing the light.

Muse of the Evening

"I know I'm not the first," I said one night,
"but tell me if I'm the best you've ever had."
Suddenly she looked a little sad.
"You're not the worst," she said. "Shut up and write."

A Tenth Anniversary Photograph, 1952

Look at their faces. You know it all.
They married the week he left for the war.
Both are gentle, intelligent people,
as all four of their parents were.

They've never talked about much
except the children. They love each other
but never wondered why they married
or had the kids or stayed together.

It wasn't because they knew the answers.
They had never heard the questions
that twisted through the jokes to come
of Moses and the Ten Suggestions.

They paid their debts and never doubted
God rewarded faith and virtue
or when you got out of line
had big and little ways to hurt you.

People walked alone in parks.
Children slept in their yards at night.
Most every man had a paying job,
and black was black and white was white.

Would you go back? Say that you can,
that all it takes is a wave and a wink
and there you are. So what do you do?
The question is crueler than you think.

Sleeping with Friends

To have someone of compatible mind
lie down with her in disarray
is not to love, but she is resigned
to a hole in the heart she never can fill
and the couple of things she knows she can find—
the needful heat that will not stay,
the independent cold that will.

To One Who Went Too Far

No use to look for signs of old affection.
Some roads run in only one direction.

Fred

Taking a husband's duties to heart
he kept her decently dressed and fed

and everything had seemed alright
till pissed again by something she said

and truly believing in the right
he whomped her up aside of the head

the way he had for all the years
they'd shared a table and a bed.

To his surprise she didn't cry
but turned and walked away instead,

went upstairs and got his gun,
took careful aim and shot him dead.

She stood with neither grin nor frown
and gazed upon him while he bled.

She managed to get him into a chair
and got herself a needle and thread

and closed the hole in the cambric shirt.
Then she got some jelly and bread

and milk and tuned the TV
to something she'd often wanted to see.

Deadsong for a Neighbor Child
Who Ran Away to the Woods

She finally found a place they couldn't find.
She wouldn't come if she could hear them call.
She knew love tore at the flesh, and flesh was all.
Stilled in breeze-blown stems and out of mind
she rode the buzzing summer, fretful fall.
She finally found a place they couldn't find.
She wouldn't come if she could hear them call.

Safe at last, unfeeling, deaf, and blind,
she lay past even peace, where countless small
and many-legg'd and legless creatures crawl.
She finally found a place they couldn't find.
She knew love tore at the flesh, and flesh was all.

On the Sacrifice of a Siamese Twin at Birth

We are one but we intended two.
Together, together we would surely have died.
Or worse, lived. Now one of us, one of us may.
But pity the hand whose closing scissors decide.

Catch with Reuben

You took for gospel what I said,
holding the glove
in just the way I said you should.
Knowing I never could teach you enough,
I thought that when you understood
how carelessly moments disappear,
your mind might hold, from a distant year,
a fading day and us still here.

No matter that your legs are short,
your arms are small,
it will all be right in time.
This arm that never threw a ball
far enough to make a team
if more than nine came out to play
threw one into your hands today
from nearly sixty years away.

The Manifold Usefulness of an Education
for Sarah and Sam and Charles
in school too far away

Geometry tells us how to tell
how far grandchildren are from here,
though this is not its only use.
It splits an angle down the middle
and calculates the hypotenuse.

Languages teach us of ancient words
with meanings like "stay" and "live" and "measure"
that hide in words we use today,
words like "distance" and "circumstance"
and "leave" and "love" and "months away."

History shows us how it was
before it became the way it is
to help us guess at what it will be.
Likewise it gives a reason to go
and sit in the shade of the family tree.

There is no subject that isn't us.
We learn, if we study with all our hearts,
that learning has a number of uses
beyond alphabets and angles
and rhymes and dates and hypotenuses.

A Visitor's Guide to the Blue Planet

Welcome to what
we kill and take
and lose and tell
and mark and make.

But Time will be a confusion
till you see parents and friends
fall to their separate ends.
With neither *will be* nor *was,*
you'll live in the present tense.

You're stuffed with days. They leave you slowly.
You'll pay no mind if people say
you'll come to feel the sun slowly
start to speed them on their way.

One day when you're naked in front of others,
playing after a bath, you'll suddenly know
—as if it were biblical knowledge—you shouldn't show
your flesh in that way, laughing, anymore.
You think you never will. You will, though.

One day you'll find yourself alone with someone else
when something not wholly your head will say, "There never was such
a mouth as this," and so you kiss and so you touch.
You'll learn there ever were such. You'll learn it again and again.
Learning will bring a sort of sadness, but not much.

Sometimes the present almost disappears
in all the up and down of the working years—
now is a place where *was* and *will be* meet,
but oh the *will be* and the *was* are sweet.

Then you'll notice something slowly.
Increasingly, you'll look around
a room, thinking of other things,
and be uncomfortably aware
that, maybe excepting a shadowy man,
a shawl in his lap, asleep in a chair,
you are the oldest person there.

Then they'll give you the shawl.
The old man won't care.
And you can have the chair.
You can have it all

till late or soon
some numberless year
there enters the room
touching your arm
one with a small
translucent voice
to say, "They're here.
They want the shawl."

Wife

Lay of the Badde Wyf

Part the first
All that she did she did not aim to do.
What she did intentionally was talk.
She had a simple hunger to say something
and see a sign that what she said was heard
by someone else, who might say, "Well" or "Maybe"
or nothing at all, but have the look of someone
to whom some words had recently been directed.

Home was where she watched the heavy hours,
each with its foggy number, grinding by.

She wanted once to work outside the home,
helping someone out somewhere for nothing.
Her husband said he would not hear of that.
She wanted once to have the kids by now.
Before the next promotion, though, and the next,
her husband would not hear of that at all.
She wanted once to join some other women
and take a morning walk around the mall,
but knew that he would never hear of that.
Her husband didn't like her being alone
with people he didn't know. Preacher, doctor,
woman down the street, it didn't matter.

She spent the day reading and running errands,
taking clothes to the cleaners and planning dinner,
paying bills and watching talk shows.
Sometimes, at night, she could imagine words
dying inside of her, empty of all their meanings.

Part the last
He ran the dry cleaners and lived above it.
"You couldn't say," he said, "it's much of a home."
She couldn't tell you why she went upstairs,
or when exactly. One day she was there.
She was surprised to see that she was there,
with new furniture and older music,
and pictures of people she never asked about.

They came with coffee first, the few stray words,
then cup by cup she told her whole life,
such as it was. And then he told her his.

She climbed the stairs repeatedly, to find
slower talk and coffee every time.
Then one day she took a glass of wine.
Then when she let his finger trace her lips
she felt something fall that she couldn't catch,
the way you feel it when you've dropped a plate.
Inside a held breath you hear it break.
All you can say is, Well, there goes a plate.

Not watching her body being released to the light,
not talking, either, she thought about her husband,
and what she was doing, and how to carry the fact,
the knowledge of it home, to make it a part
of pancakes and bills and looking for car keys.

Then she smiled, lying back in the light of her thoughts,
suddenly seeing how ascending the stairs
and drinking the wine and being naked there
would surely be among the numberless things
he himself would say he'd never hear of.   *FORBIDS*
So let him never hear, for who was she,   *HER ?*
unfaithful wife, to doubt his wisdom now?

Beside an Open Grave
the Mind of the Young Preacher
Comes Almost to Terms

They came to hear what they have the right to hear.
They're circling now for sure and certain knowledge.
If I can tell them nothing but what I know,
I can begin by describing my present discomfort
and tell them in closing how to spell my name.

I want to tell them what they want to hear.
If what they want to hear may not be true,
there's truth enough in knowing they want to hear it.

How are we sure of so little after so long?

Stop this stuff. We need a requiem here.
See, now, how silence pours from all their faces.

Well, then. Open your mouth. Begin. Begin . . .

    . . . So let us begin to pray.
    All language is requiem.
    Someday someone will grieve
    for us who grieve today
    and then someone for them
    as class by class we leave
    where none could dare to stay.
    Not for us to condemn,
    defend, or beg reprieve,
    or praise too much, but say,
    O Lord, receive. Receive.

Jonathan in Awe

    Jonathan walking, careful of every crack,
    pausing to watch the supper traffic pass,
    works through the list of mysteries in his mind:
    that teakwood, when it breaks, will shatter like glass;
    that no one knows from where the music came
    to which we sing the words of *Amazing Grace;*
    that no one is ever told what anyone tells;
    that God, in the beginning, had only three ways
    to express Itself—make nothing, or something else,
    or make all this, where Jonathan saunters once.

At breakfast alone he thinks of how it is,
that when he is near the woman that he wants
with only a gnomic hope to raise its head,
he feels soprano, naked, and two feet tall.

Such are things of varied immediacy
that hold the mind of Jonathan in thrall,
no matter how much he longs for the mayfly thoughts
he had as a child to return and busy his head
when he is walking, stepping over cracks,
or pulling the blankets up on his narrow bed.

Jonathan Entertaining

Jonathan has invited all his friends
and says to those who come and lift their glasses
a second time for an old year as it ends,
a first time for a new one, "How time passes!"

He adds for conversation how one spends
the first gradual years, slow as molasses,
knowing nothing of what the world intends,
the middle years discussing gains and losses,

the later years not talking much of gains,
a bit of the victories children's children win,
but mostly of holding steady against the pains
of coming to terms and coming apart within.

Leaving, his friends do as they've done before.
Shaking hands and shaking heads together,
they pause two by two at the open door,
agreeing that life is hardly worth the bother,

leaving the wadded napkins, splattered floor,
the broken plate to Jonathan, who would rather
have eaten a mouse than stand a minute more
to watch each woman go and a man go with her.

Alone, he half suspects they *don't* agree,
not one, as if he'd shown a slide show
of a trip to places they didn't want to go,
with towns and mountains they didn't care to see,
and didn't have the heart to tell him so.

Jonathan Confronts the Question

He knows there are those who say you can never know
and he'd always assumed that this was true,
but exceedingly sad one night he suddenly knew
that God set up the whole thing for show,
then saw he had no one to show it to.

And now so God won't have to have the same
old audience all the time, we have to die,
filing out of the rows we occupy
more or less in the order in which we came.
Wave as you will, you'll never catch his eye.

Jonathan Losing

They cheered when he started out and kept it up,
took his colors and wore them as their own.
Go, they said. *Go.* He knew as soon as he failed
that he could have done it if they had left him alone.

Jonathan Happy

He'd never—though he saw the failing—
truly understood
how to know if he was feeling
bad or feeling good,

the former seemed so like the latter.
He laughs to know he sees,
pouring out a bag of litter,
spraying for ticks and fleas.

Heating his soup, he likes to keep
an eye upon the creature
curled on the arm of the couch asleep.
He loves their common nature,

that neither has anywhere to go,
both apparently willing
to rest in silence with things they know
that neither is skilled at telling.

Jonathan Seduced

He doesn't know what she wants or why she stays
as one by two by three the crowd thins.
He holds his folded papers and says, No,
he doesn't always know when he begins

where he might end up. Her, too, she says,
although she's practically done nothing at all
compared to him. What happens after that,
or if she tells him her name, he can't recall,

except for blinks of time, strobe-like scenes,
hands everywhere and flashes of long flesh,
almost like photos in all those magazines
he looks at when he has to. A suddenly fresh

expectant face, far from a circle of friends,
may make him remember where the memory hid,
and sometimes going to sleep, but he mostly intends
to know that it never took place till it never did.

Jonathan's Secret

Jonathan doesn't know how to tell a lie.
It's a handicap. He doesn't know how to say,
if anybody says, Do you like this thing?
when he doesn't at all, that he likes it anyway.

He knows that people think of him as honest.
In this he feels dishonest. Truth to tell,
he thinks he'd like to lie. He thinks he envies
people who do it sparingly and well.

He puts the words together but they won't stay.
It looks like shit, he says. He never intends
to hurt anybody. He'd lie, if he knew how,
his tongue loose to have some faithful friends.

Jonathan in Mourning

Beside the grave, a bottle in his hand,
Jonathan tells himself that from the start—
not giving a thought to where the thought will land—
from even before the murky pulling apart

of autocatalytical carbon rings,
till suns reclaim their planets in the end,
nothing happens twice and most things
never happen at all. "I don't intend

a eulogy here," he sighs, squatting down.
"A brief configuration has fallen away,
and what is less dependable than a noun?"
Lifting his bottle up to the fading day

he thinks about how barely he is here
and brings the bottle down for a long drink.
Bushes around the yard come darkly near
as the air turns chill and he watches the sun sink.

He says to the bottle, taking another pull,
"It's strange that anything is anywhere . . .
it's sad to feel what I felt when you were full,"
and forms what might have been heard as a kind of prayer.

"Lord knows it was law, back before things began,
that everything that is, is the only one,
a cat as unrepeatable as a man,
so now there are reasons enough and now there are none."

He thinks that tomorrow he might cut back a little.
Trees are creeping toward him across the lawn.
He drains the last swallow from the bottle.
"I've got to go in," he says. "Poor Kitty. Poor Jon."

Jonathan Aging

Jonathan feels like a character out of Dickens.
He's served foods he can't digest anymore.
He feels things move that never have moved before.
His graying hair grows thin and his body thickens.

He thinks of mortality more than he used to.
He knows his friends have seen how his flesh is soft,
that he has neither time nor interest left
to do the few things that he used to do.

He finds time for another glass of scotch
before dinner, is still surprised to hold
the paper so far away and misread his watch.

If it confuses him how people grow old
to curse the lapsing of the heart and crotch,
it was never a secret and he was certainly told.

Jonathan at Last

He thinks of when he is dead and how it will be,
of how a colleague could say, or maybe a neighbor,
being by every convention laudatory
within the limits of truth and good grace,
that if there was little enough of grandeur and glory
still he suggested something of Rome and Greece.
Or, failing that, someone could rise and say
that he was often remarkably civilized
for a man who lived alone in constant dismay
in a large house where couples came to the door
prepared to tell him why they couldn't stay;
who had a cat, as brief as it was small,
and once a brittle hope, briefer than that,
and little help or comfort ever at all.

She Talks to Her Sister, Briefly By
on the Way to West Memphis

It's been four years now, come October five.
You're sure you won't have another bite?
There's plenty more. I did look forward to it,
the day he wouldn't have to go to work.
But listen to me. Not even getting married
can change a life like having him underfoot.

That's him hammering something in the basement.
He's built himself a workshop, thank the Lord,
else he'd be here with me all the time,
talking and talking with nothing to talk about.

There aren't a lot of things that need repair
about a house like this, the two of us,
so we end up—I guess a little surprised—
reading the newspapers, eating in silence,
and finally talking again in spite of ourselves.

It wouldn't behoove me at all to fault him for this.
He's doing what we planned for him to do.
He truly is the salt, you know, of the earth.
There's not a negative thing worthy of notice
that I or anybody could say about him.

Years ago once, when I was doing the laundry,
I found a phone number stuck in a pocket,
a local number in someone else's hand
written on the edge of a paper napkin.
It was the napkin set my nose to itching.
Half of me didn't want me to but I called it.
A woman said hello and I hung up.
I didn't know what to say. She might have been
the wife or daughter of one of the men he worked with.

Well, that was back a long time ago.

The time when people ought to be together
night and day like this, day and night,
are those first years, when nothing seems enough.
Not now, when a brushing touch can do for a day.

What this does, you know, it makes it harder
for one to go on alone when the other dies.
You get too used to being half of something.

He traded himself in for what he's got.
I suppose it shakes some wrinkles out,
stopping a way of living and starting another.
I wouldn't know. I'm doing the life I've done
for more than forty years, except that now
I can't talk to myself the way I did.
He thinks I'm talking to him, and I ought to be.

Sometimes I think, Who is this person I'm wearing?
I can't recall the last time I sat
and stared at the wall as long as I wanted to.

Still, I know, I might have spent those years
with some sad man who lacked imagination
to know the difference between the truth and fact,
who never said, when he heard a siren start,
that someone's plans for the day had come undone.

Listen. Here he comes. He'll want to show us
something he's put together or taken apart.
He'll want to set it down where we can see it.
Sometimes it is remarkable what he does.
I think he thinks that everything is fine.
I've never said a word of this to him,
so you can see now what the problem is.
If he doesn't have the good sense to see
that I don't care for anything anymore,
including him and whatever he has in his hands,
if he doesn't have the sense to see that,
what is he going to do if I die first?

The Young Instructor Talks to Himself
Winding Up the Semester

So then she will go away. And what's the loss?
Thinking of love is more and loving is less

than we have wanted to say. So let her go.
Someone twisting her hair in the back row

will take her place, one with benevolent lips,
her eyes at times betraying a little lapse

of what she calls attention, vaguely gazing
into the middle distance. You will be praising

her lips and hair and eyes in the same bed
where each one seemed to put her pretty head.

Again when morning comes she'll sit in class
twisting her hair to make the minutes pass.

You'll think this time she might almost recall
the sass, the nakedness, the long caress,
but you can see in her eyes that she doesn't at all.

Clutter of Silence: Invention for Two Voices

You ought to see him there in the backyard
standing like a stump. About sundown,
he wanders out and tosses a rock or two.
A squirrel could nest in a pocket and he wouldn't know it.
He used to tell me what he'd done all day.
I'd let him talk then tell him how I felt,
the sun going down, but he would never listen.
The day his sister died he crashed the car
so he could know that he was feeling something.
Nothing seems real to him till he acts it out.
We haven't laid down for love in a long time.
We didn't do it together when we did it.
Not really together, I mean, him looking down,
me looking up, the ceiling fan turning,
his body telling both of us when to stop.
Do I still love him? I'd like to say I do.
I worry about him when he has to travel.
I guess I'd worry about anybody
that shared a house with me for thirty years.
Does he love me, though? That might be the question.
He sits for hours without saying a word
and never likes anything I fix.

You ought to stand where I do, out in the yard.
Watch any window and there she'll be, in the bedroom,
lights off and on, the dining room and kitchen,
like if she sat for a second something would get her.
She thinks I don't pay attention but I do.
When I get home from work I always ask her,
What did you do today? and she says, Nothing.
Doing, doing, all the time doing,
and never caring to tell me what she does.
She gained ten pounds of grief when her mother died.
That's when it came to me like a bumper sticker,
her flesh is just feelings in disguise.
It never had a purpose all its own.
We've come to not make love much anymore.
She doesn't care and I can live without it.
We did it once the way the movies do it,
but then she started watching the ceiling fan.
Do I love her? Who else might I love
if I don't love her? We're talking thirty years.
You could turn that question around to her,
who gets mad with no warming up
and puts oregano on everything.

Jonah on His Deathbed

I was ready long before this day.
You've read that I was, but save for the barest facts
you don't know half the story from where I stood.

It wasn't hard to see why He picked me out.
I was a good Jew and free to travel.
Also, being a prophet—though I grant you,
not well known till all this came to pass—
I was prepared to see the ways of God
and make them known in well-crafted phrases
the Lord would lay in my mouth. I'd done it before,
on small assignments, and done it very well.

Most of the time we saw eye-to-eye,
but why the Lord should attend to Nineveh
was something I thought deserved a little discussion.
I made a list. For one, the Ninevites
are ignorant. For two, they're happy so.
For three, they pose a constant threat to peace.
If that was not enough, I meant to mention
what an embarrassment to humankind
they are, whose only art is arrogance.
And what would other prophets think about me
running off to visit such a people?
Would anyone believe that God had sent me?
Of course He did! And can't you see them grinning?

I failed to see what good it was going to do.
"Tell them I'll overthrow them," He said. Sure.
"A month and ten days," He said. Right.
Then He'd probably spare them, whatever happened,
and there I'd be, looking like a fool.

So what the heck, I thought, a little side trip
till He gets interested in something else.
Maybe Tarshish, down the coast of Spain,
a little mining town run by Jews
who surely needed to hear the word of God
and had at least the blood to understand it.

I only had to go as far as Joppa
to come on a foreign ship prepared to sail.

I was sleeping the sleep of a clear conscience,
two days out and not a word from the Lord,
when the storm hit. The sailors woke me up.
I can tell you they were terrified,
the sky black and the sails about to rip.
Up on the deck we cast lots, to learn
which one among us God was angry with.
Can you believe it? There on a lurching ship,
breakers nearly as high as the creaking mast,
each of us shaking a bunch of chicken bones.
Of course they pointed to me every time.
I wanted to say they had rigged the whole thing
but I knew better. I knew what I had to do.

God would have drowned the lot of them to get me.
He doesn't have to answer to anyone,
but I was not about to stand before him
with twenty drowned Phoenicians on my hands.
I told the men to toss me overboard.
I lacked the nerve to jump, and on that count
I'll thank you not to judge.

                    I have to say
I saw more compassion in their eyes
than I had heard in the voices of the Lord
since this began. They bent themselves to the oars,
which I took as a kindness and still do,
but soon it was clear that I would have to go.

Wrapped in the fish, I knew what he wanted to hear,
but I think I was madder than he was.
I decided I wasn't going to say it.

There in the slime, though, the smell and the darkness,
I said the words. I said, "My Lord, I love you."
I said it twice again, and He let me out.
And then I got myself to Nineveh.

You can imagine that I was in no mood
to hold forth. I told them what He said:
"You've all got forty days, and that's it."
Then every one of them saw the light at once
and went home and changed to sackcloth.
I half-suspected God was playing games.
The king heard, and he ordered the people to fast.
Also, the dogs and donkeys and cattle and sheep
were not to have any food or water at all.
They also had to go in sackcloth.

God said they seemed a nice bunch of people
who demonstrated remorse and He wouldn't hurt them.
I knew that's what He would say and He knew I knew it.

I can tell you, it put a strain on things.
I yelled and tore my clothes. "Go on," I said,
"and finish me off." Then I got out of there.
I walked as far as I could. When it got too hot
I settled myself down on the side of a hill
to see if the Ninevites would mess it up.
That was where He truly became unkind.

First, a gourd grew up and blocked the sun,
which at first I took as a nice gesture.
But then He sent a worm into the plant
and the plant died. And then the sun and the wind
bore into my brain. "Just go ahead and kill me,"
that's all I said. The Lord spoke in thunder,
"What have you got to be so angry about?"

That's the line that did it. He knew well enough.
I slapped my forehead and tore my clothes some more.
Then He said, "Look. Try to feel some pity.
These Ninevites are not very smart,
and think of all the cattle I would have killed
if you had not come and I had stricken the land."

Sure, I thought, and what about dogs and sheep
and donkeys with no water for more than a day?

But, as the story is written, I did not answer.
What could I say, sitting there in the sun?
That this was all for show and out of fear?
He loves them both.

I truly meant to die.
He wouldn't have it. Who knows the ways of the Lord?
Perhaps it gives Him pleasure to have me here
telling this story again. What else can I do?
Think what it's like with half your life to live
and known as the one who used to be the prophet
that God chose to send to Nineveh.

So much for me. You want to know something else?
After the squeezing gut, after the stink,
three days inside the fish, after the awful
courtesy on the ship, what I think of most
are the animals under that sun, with nothing to drink.

Coming Out

How could I have told you except to tell you?
I half-suspected you knew for a long time.
We wear each other's clothes. You must have known.
I thought you'd say, So let me call the papers,
or something like that. I'm sorry. I did it badly.

I thought the only thing to worry about
was how my folks will take it when I tell them.

My father can't even bring himself to believe
I'd want to love a man, much less a woman.
I'd give the whole world to have them tell me
it won't make any difference, but it will.

Even to you it does. You're afraid of me, right?
OK, you're not. You want a medal or something?

Hey, if you cry you're going to make me cry.
I told myself I wouldn't. So here we go,
both wet again, two kids at a frigging movie.

So look at this. Imagine how you'd feel
if almost everyone you knew was gay
and everyone called you queer if you were not,
if all TV and novels and billboards
had women loving women and men, men.
Think of telling someone you wanted a man.

My father will leave the house and sit somewhere.
My mother will go into the kitchen and clean something.

Remember when we hung around the high school
talking with all the girls about the boys?
I would go home and hit my hand with a stick
to make it stop wanting what it wanted.

Then gradually you learn to say the word.
The first person you have to tell is yourself.

Then more and more, whenever I lied to hide it,
it was only the lying I was ashamed of.

So don't think I don't like myself. I do.
You're never going to make it if you don't.
Imagine saying every day in the mirror,
Shame on you. What if your parents knew?

I've thought about my parents a long time
but finally I thought about their daughter.

When I was little and I was all dressed up
for church or something my mother would look and say,
"You're going to make somebody a fine wife."

"Just put those thoughts away," my father would laugh.
"She'll never have to hunt for board and bed."
He'd lay his paper down and give me a hug.
"Are you going to leave your daddy for some other man?"
Maybe he can remember that now,
how happy it made him feel when I shook my head.

Holiday Inn: Surrounded by Someone Else's Reunion
He Comes to Terms

for George Haley and the others

The large marquee said, Welcome Family Winston.
One N was upside down. Nobody cared.
From nearly black to almond, stroller to cane,
with license plates from Pennsylvania to Texas,
they filled the pool and parking lot with laughter.
They filled the lobby and both the elevators.

I made small conversation with a few
who might remember singing some of the songs,
holding awhile a hand as white as mine.
Most who were younger than that, whenever I spoke,
shut their faces down and turned away.

One man with hair like gray-white rolling clouds
spoke kindly once. I left him to such a silence
I thought of old pictures, collaborators in France
ostracized and having their heads shaved.

As if I had not marched, and ridden, and sat,
and held hands and sung. But what should that buy me?

I had a dream in which a black child
said, "Papa, all those people look the same."

I won't say they were for nothing, the years together.
Lord knows we lost, but it was a good game.

228

Showing Late Symptoms She First Tries to Fix
Herself in the Minds of Her Children

I try to take them where they want to go
but not to let them have their way too much.
I try to play their games, but not so much
I make them uneasy, making a fool of myself.
I cook what they like when I can. I tell them I love them.
I tell them too often, though, and they don't hear me.

If there's a chance that one of them might remember,
it won't be the baby. His brother's six and a half.
The little one won't be five for seven months.

But then I've thought, If I could plant something
that might come to blossom far in the future,
if I could find an odor, something rare,
something they might not smell on anyone else,
something no teacher or friend's mother would wear,
if I could afford it, then maybe in twenty years
one of my sons would say to some young woman
in some distant city, "Nothing. It's nothing.
Something made me think about my mother."

Wouldn't that beat all, me suddenly there?
Not knowing of course or caring, but still there,
a kind of ghost, just floating in the room.

They're still so young, though, their hands are so small.
I don't want to haunt them. They're wearing my flesh.
They'll cry me slowly away at bedtime.

But that would be something, the woman pretty and all.

From *The Ways We Touch*

Part I: Rumors

Listen

I threw a snowball across the backyard.
My dog ran after it to bring it back.
It broke as it fell, scattering snow over snow.
She stood confused, seeing and smelling nothing.
She searched in widening circles until I called her.

She looked at me and said as clearly in silence
as if she had spoken,
I know it's here, I'll find it,
went back to the center and started the circles again.

I called her two more times before she came
slowly, stopping once to look back.

That was this morning. I'm sure that she's forgotten.
I've had some trouble putting it out of my mind.

A Lesson on the Twentieth Century

They rode around in auto-mobiles,
metal sitting rooms that sat on wheels
and coursed a network of concrete
laid down by labor, a grid of street across street
inside the cities, and on the countryside
long winding ribbons sometimes laid so wide
eight of the units could run along together,
half going one direction and half the other.
The engines that powered them were built to burn
the residue of ancient life. You'll learn
now if you will activate your screens
how the drivers of these ingenious machines
could shift the ratios of their mechanical gears.
A lot of things have altered over the years
since nations went to war for gods and lands
and things lived in the oceans and there were bands
of people who used their own breath and hands
to make their music. All this was long before
we freed ourselves from fretting about chance
and learned not to walk too close to the shore
or think about things like dolphins anymore.

It Came to Pass on a Planet
Third from a Minor Sun in a Solar System
Out on the Edge of One of the Galaxies

If there are intelligent beings
in some other place
did Jesus go to be born
and die for them there?

If he didn't
are they still offered the grace
of God and if they aren't
is that fair?

Autopsy

Here in a place where much
was hated and held dear
you feel no part of yes
no matter what you touch.

There isn't a soul here,
only an empty house in a brambly lot.
But is there not a forwarding address?
No, there is not.

Woman with Dog

Walking along a beach on St. George Island
where two men fished for sea trout under the surf
he saw the track of a dog with paws so big
it must have weighed a hundred pounds or more,
a trail so narrow no print was out of line
by half its width. You don't often see, he said,
a dog like that, of such great weight and grace.

There joined and left and crossed the track of the dog
the deep meandering prints of someone running,
more loping than jogging—the feet fell farther apart,
the heels sunk into the sand a little more deeply.
The shoes were new, by their treads, and smaller than his.

With legs too long for a child, this was a woman,
a woman running, but less intent than her dog
on getting where they were going. And where was that?
And who was waiting there, to tell her what?
How glad would she be to be home, getting into the shower?

The prints were new, the newest on the beach.
No wave or wind or seabird track had touched them.
He tightened his eyes, wanting to see them running
and thought he did, maybe, against a dune
as far as he could focus. He saw something,
a group of gulls rising, and then nothing.

He looked for the trail to end at tire tracks
where blacktop curved into the beach, but it kept on going,
into the evening, farther than he could go
if he was going to be where he said he'd be
for dinner and talk and a fireplace and people he knew.
Already, when he turned back, the two men fishing
seemed so small in the distance they could have been driftwood.
Somewhere behind him the woman, not thinking of him.
Near the closed door, asleep, the magnificent dog.

A Thought as It Turns

Truly we have not been here long—twelve hours,
if you consider the age of the earth a year;
by the age of the universe, the beat of a heart.
That's likely half the time we'll have here
before we tuck it in and call it a day.

We sometimes feel uneasy, looking forward,
but won't feel too bad, maybe, looking back
to where, if we never outgrew our temper and fear,
and visions left us blind and voices deaf,
still there was art a while, and math, and music,
forbearance and hope and wit and architecture,
and once this porch, and once this day, and you
at needlepoint slowly, guiding the needle through.

10,000-Year-Old Tree Discovered
Shades Two and Half Acres

This tree took root before Jerusalem,
before Troy, before Constantinople,
before there were cities to name,
before there were farms,
the most ancient living thing on earth
for all we know,
which may mean also in the universe.
So listen to this and tell me
how it grabs you:

Come let us open the door
to your new home
where you can lead your guests across a floor
older than Rome.

I think Jerusalem is older but it doesn't rhyme.
Anyway, poets use Rome to mean a really long time.

He Shuts His Eyes
for the Layman's Long Prayer about Lust
and the Mind of the Young Preacher
Wanders Again

Say a man tells a woman that he was blind
from birth and lately found a medical chance
to see it and took it.
Say this is a lie he tells, a little pretense.

He means he therefore has the eyes of a child,
not having seen a woman naked. He knows
what she will do.
She is going to take off all her clothes.

Will he be blind in hell? Surely he will,
though will it matter when he's all afire?
Say there's a child.
The child did neither pleasure nor conspire

but guilt follows the flesh. His ancient book
will fall out of balance if God forgets.
No matter to Him
how hard we pray, God please, He collects His debts.

Pure love has little use for sentiment
and hope, if you live forever, must seem odd,
though maybe He tries
to love the ways we love. Please God.

At the Christening of an Infant
the Mind of the Young Preacher
Wanders Again

It's not for us to give this soul to God.
We're here to recognize that the soul is God's.
Rather, I want to say, the soul is God.
This is as doubtless and clear as the baby's eyes.

What swirls about me when I hold a thing
so recently a fish, a tadpole,
is a murky and restless thought: when came the soul?
It had to be at a moment. It couldn't have been
little by little. The mind is repelled, rebels
at the thought of sort of a soul, God tiptoeing in.

A sperm and an egg, each with half a soul,
is something equally noxious, when you consider
the countless that go for nothing.

Say the zygote,
the fertilized egg, gets a soul for the fact of that—
what if it doesn't grab hold and falls in the toilet?
Does that soul get another chance? If not,
where does it go? What does it know about being?

At viability, then? Is that the word?
And what exactly is that? Eleven-thirteen
on the second day of the twenty-fourth week?
I don't know if God can tell time.

I know there is a soul in this mass of cells.
I think I know when it leaves. May that be a long
and richly textured time from all of this.

Take our love and your chances. Take all your names,
your new one, and God, and human—and go forth.

The Affair

He lived in a double-wide and drove a truck,
drank a Pepsi-Cola at every meal,
read the obituaries and comic strips,
meant the center of everything he said,
listened to country music, laughed at jokes,
and bet a little on the football spread.

She lived in a high-rise and practiced law,
had coffee at breakfast, always three and black,
read the obituaries and business news,
meant both sides of everything she said,
listened to new jazz, smiled at wit,
and bet on the futures market, the price spread.

They spoke the same language, more or less,
but not to each other, of course, except for the time
when they were stuck alone in an elevator
for fifty minutes five years ago.
Though each was afraid of needing a bathroom
they both behaved the way they felt befit
the sudden circumstance. They tried to relax.
She totally missed his jokes and he her wit.

Now, though, making love to the dwindling few,
he thinks of her, the small hands and the scent.
In bed she imagines him, the mouth and the smell,
what he would want her to do, what he would do.

The Light in the Eyes

Who knows
where it goes?

Part 2: Errands

On Word That the Old Children's Stories
Have Been Brought Up to Date

The farmer's wife missed the tails entirely.
Jack and the giant became the best of friends.
The boy cried *wolf* again and the people came
but didn't hurt the wolf, just sent it thence.

Young Ms. Hubbard's cupboard was full of bones.
Humpty Dumpty bounced like a rubber ball.
The woman who lived in a shoe was kind to her kids.
Ms. Muffet was not afraid of spiders at all.

So now does Icarus flutter down to the sea
and swim ashore? Does Cyclops keep his eye?
Doesn't Achilles worry about his heel?
Are there no consequences? Does no one die?

Is this what we say to the kids—You can be bad,
but, hey, it's OK. Nobody's going to get mad?

Personals

Like a challenge? Male, 45
could pass for 60, at least twice divorced,
heavy smoker, sober now and then,
living in trailer home with no water,
looking for female with good job.

We may have no more need for half our doctors
and every talk show will fold flat
when we can understand why there are people
who will enclose a picture and answer that.

Romance

First, of course, you think of Robin Hood,
partial to poor folk, unimpressed by power;
then the cat burglar, black slacks and sweater,
always unarmed, making clever remarks.
Then someone steps suddenly out of an alley
to take your cash and the ring that meant so much,
or the car has disappeared from the carport,
or you get home and someone has emptied the house
you promised to pay for in thirty years.
You imagine you have them in court. They show you hells,
bad fathers and broken homes, their mothers' tears.
They can die now, you say, or die in their cells.

Her, Though

It didn't come all at once, it didn't come easy,
deciding to try to find the off button.

It wasn't the humiliation of stumbling along
a murky neuron path looking for names
of people he saw every day. It wasn't the pain,
though more and more he imagined pans of water
boiling behind his eyeballs, his liver grilled.

Her, though, having to handle it all by herself
that's what it was. He thought and thought about it,
all the attention and money to be paid,
then her watching him fade to a poor suggestion
of something in her past. He was more afraid
of luring her into that than surprising her now
when he and the bank account both had a balance.

He thought of little else but doing it.
He wasn't sure that these were dark thoughts.
If they were dark he had them anyway,
though now and then he smiled or nearly smiled
to think of what doing it used to mean
in maybe the backseat of a Chevrolet
with what-was-her-name with the sweet-smelling hair,
something he'd thought about and thought about
the long year when he was seventeen,
something that somehow never did work out.

A Good Son

He called home every once in a while
to tell his mother,
just so he could imagine how she would smile,
something or other

about a girlfriend
or work or a new movie he might have seen,
whatever was right.
He lied some, but mostly he stayed between

fantasy and fact.
He was a good son. He loved his mother a lot
and knew what she needed—
to live through him whether he lived or not.

The Sissy

He's never been pointed to first for anything
except by the bony finger of the teacher
who knows he'll have his homework done and perfect
which makes him so ashamed he'd like to fail
but knows that failing would leave him here even longer.

He tries to catch a ball and he wants to die.
Sometimes he lies in bed and thinks of dying,
forcing out some last important words
just before his head falls back on the pillow
or rolls out of the hand of whoever holds it
onto the carpet or grass or saddle blanket
leaving those people that never knew who he was
to look at one another in dusty silence.

A Christmas Poem

In a little bar on the Gulf Coast
someone offers a Christmas toast.
The piano player, believe it or not,
plays "As Time Goes By." Almost.

The bartender brings over a lot
of nuts and crackers. I have a shot
of Jack to get me on my way.
After a while, it's *What have you got?*

A drunk counts out some coins to pay
for a bottle of wine. He stops to say,
How are you doing? The syllables stink.
I lift my glass to say, I'm OK.

Out of the corner what I think
is a man in a wig and a ratty mink
weaves his way across the floor
and buys the piano player a drink.

At a table for two close to the door
a man seems to mean to ignore
a woman chewing a wad of gum.
The bartender brings me a couple more.

The piano player plays us some
of what the season wants. We hum
along and call for more and then
a man at the bar takes his thumb

out of his mouth and says there are ten
minutes left, Good will to men.
Good men, a woman says, to me.
He puts his thumb in his mouth again.

I manage a toast to the Christmas tree
and one to the sweet absurdity
of the miracle of the verb to be.
Lucky you, lucky me.

71 *South*

He thinks he wouldn't have thought for all those miles
about the squirrel but shrugged and said, Tough luck,
if it hadn't been for the acorn he saw in its mouth
when it turned confused to face the truck.

As You Both Shall Live

I'm sorry, I'm really just too tired tonight.
I think she's a little young to have a date.
I don't see how we can afford that.
It's fine. I just don't have any appetite.
I thought we'd watch it together. It starts at eight.
I still don't understand what you're getting at.
There are things I can do and things I can't.
It's been longer than that. Like a couple of weeks.
I told you about it. You said to go ahead.
She's just someone I know. She works at the plant.
I thought you fixed it. Listen. It still squeaks.
In one of those boxes probably under the bed.
I still don't understand what you're getting at.
You ought to tell the doctor about your cough.
She's going to be with people we don't know.
I just can't believe you did that.
Three more men on the shift have been laid off.
Let the dog back in before you go.

For J. William Fulbright
on the Day of His Death

Walking the square in a tree-thick mountain town
in Arkansas, a visitor is shown
a face and a few words, a monument
in bronze and stone,

a good and visible and local sign
of all the good he left us, something to touch,
but other monuments will last as long
and say as much.

Think of students with minds made darkly rich
by cultures not their own, and who can say—
given the sweet contagion of a thought—
how far away

the tremors of opening minds may resonate?
Beyond our great-grandchildren? Farther than that?
Socrates taught young Plato at whose student's feet
we all have sat

through forty increasingly nervous centuries
while those rare minds turned other minds around.
Then think of the hundreds of nations, talking and talking,
the endless sound

of words, words, in every language words,
old terrible words but better than bombs by far.
This brave cacophony, he brought about.
All that we are—

fumbling and noble, enduring, uncertain, and weak—
this body of nations embodies: the foulest and best,
imperfect memory, fear, the one long hope,
and the half-expressed

deep rage of half the world, brought barely together:
one simple resolution, his gift to earth;
some words, when we had little faith in what
words could be worth.

Then think that every time, alone in darkness,
someone finds the courage to take a stand
against the arrogance of power or lifts
one hesitant hand

against the tyranny of mad momentum,
there is a monument. And there. And there.
And there, in a thought that seems at times too simple
for us to bear,

that peace is a progress moving first in the mind,
something left a little more clear
in the heads of the heads of state and common people
because he was here.

What shall we say, now that he's not among us?
We might speak for a moment as if he were.
We might take once his imagined hand and say,
We'll miss you, sir.

Wide Place in the Road

At last when he had to go back
to be at one of those funerals he had to attend,
he knew how it would be,
hugging his aunts and asking about a friend

he hadn't thought of in years,
everyone saying he surely was a sight
for sore eyes and such,
how kind he was to come. But he found a seat

alone on the back bench.
He watched the dresses, the plodding blue overalls,
the white shirts stiffly clean,
new canvas shoes on all the whispering girls.

The preacher kept on saying,
"Eternal bliss awaits you and I."
Then he saw with discomfort
that only he and the preacher wore a tie.

He thought of slipping it off,
wadding it into his pocket, but then he thought, No.
He had to be what he was,
not what his father was too long ago.

Aunts and uncles and cousins,
he wasn't sure that these were why he came,
or why, since he had come,
it somehow made him nervous to put his name

in the little book at the door,
or if he imagined the looks of reprimand.
He had a long drive home.
If he didn't stop at the grave they would understand.

Quantum Theory Made Simple

He knew he had another thirty years
and that's if he was lucky. He might have less
but that didn't bother him much. He had his turn.
One death in an endless turning was little loss.

The pattern stayed, the tapestry went on,
and buried somewhere in the warp and weave
some twist of a thread would say that he was here
if only long enough to stand and wave

and step away. He went gladly to work
and worked his deals as if he didn't care
that he was temporary. He watched the news
and loved his wife and bought a bigger car.

But when he learned that all the universe,
now like a spreading hand, would close to a fist
in a billion years then disappear completely,
he knew that he'd been tricked. He'd never faced

the prospect of a time past all of time
with no one left to wonder about the days
when he was here, to marvel at old bones
the way he did but now no longer does.

Now, driving home, he thinks how silly cars are,
how useless it is, and necessary, now that he's here,
to take the garbage out, and brush his teeth,
and cover up the gray in his thinning hair.

If Ever There Was One

She could tell he loved her. He wanted her there
sitting in the front pew when he preached.
He liked to watch her putting up her hair
and ate whatever she cooked and never broached

the subject of the years before they met.
He was thoughtful always. He let her say
whether or not they did anything in bed
and tried to learn the games she tried to play.

She could tell how deep his feeling ran.
He liked to say her name and bought her stuff
for no good reason. He was a gentle man.
How few there are she knew well enough.

He sometimes reached to flick away a speck
of something on her clothes and didn't drum
his fingers on the table when she spoke.
What would he do if he knew she had a dream

sometimes, slipping out of her nightgown—
if ever God forbid he really knew her—
to slip once out of the house and across town
and find someone to talk dirty to her.

Ballad of a Little Delta Town

They said their vows in the Church of the Pentecost
and she had blushed a little when they kissed.
She'd got her a good man, who everyone knew
would do most anything you asked him to.
He fought the fire when the neighbor's toolshed burned
and wasn't the last to call the time he learned
a distant relative had come to harm,
but he had difficulty being warm.
He sometimes said the words but they sounded flat.
At first she sort of pitied him for that.
She told herself she was lucky to have his love
and a double-wide, that it was blessing enough
just to touch his hand as she fell asleep.
Year by year, though, as the chill ran deep,
she felt her feelings harden and grow brittle.
She took a job to be out of the house a little.

In the only café in the twelve-block delta town
a man lumbered up to the counter and spraddled down.
She brought him coffee and wiped the counter clean.
He talked like someone out of a magazine.
He was as sure of himself as a true believer,
smart as a quarterback, quick as a wide receiver.
Smarter than many, she'd always thought she knew
the way to read the winds, however they blew,
and knew as she knew her name that nothing is free
but took his touch for the truth it seemed to be.

Between a stand of maple and lowing cows
she felt for leaves in her hair and buttoned her blouse.
He took his 18-wheeler out of town.

What's done is done, she said. She let herself down
as carefully as she could to her frightening door,
thinking of what she wasn't anymore.

She put her nightgown on and sat on the bed.
Half the glass of bleach fell over the spread.

Her husband found her lying in a sprawl
as if the bed had caught her in a fall.

When neighbors and kin leaned toward him in his loss
he leaned away. Someone standing across
from where he stood at the coffin might have said
that he looked sad or not at all sad,
that his lower lip tightened and started to curl
much like the lip of a person thinking cruel
thoughts or someone trying not to cry,
and no one heard him say, Good-bye, good-bye.

An Old Man Leaves His Church for the Last Time

It's all about tithing now.

What happened to the gospel way
of getting saved?

Before, when people got saved
they stopped doing the way they used to do.
They had new ways to live,
not a part of this world.

Today people say they're going
to live like Christians
but still they go to dances,
they go to movies,
still they live the way they used to live.

How do they ever expect to shine their light?

Jesus wants us to witness by words and works
and also how we dress.

The Bible tells us, "Be ye separate people."

And where is the preacher of holiness or hell?
Before, whenever sinners came to church
there was a pulling spirit, they felt something.
Now it's nothing but altar committees
and tithing.

Let me tell you, it's holiness or hell.

I know I get on the nerves
of worldly people.

Let me ask you, though,
if you were standing alone at the edge of town
and saw a rolling dust cloud coming toward you
what kind of a person would you be
if you didn't call out in the streets
that a cloud was coming?

Part 3: Admonitions

For All Our Great-Grandchildren

                          when they are grown
with eyes and names I wish I could have known
and more real now than I, but how to begin
speaking to you, our sweet and future kin?

You're each the only one there is of you.
This is not to tell you something new,
but think about the responsibility
of being the only one you will ever be.
Treat your mind and body with the care
you ought to spend on anything that rare.

Forgive yourself. No other forgiving is more
necessary or harder to beg for.

Be nearly too stubborn to change, but never quite.
Be kind, when you can. When you cannot, be right.

Live with the knowledge that living takes its toll
till soon or late we spin out of control,
regardless of obligation, love, or law.

Wherever you are, the moon or Arkansas,
I felt you close today. Don't pay much mind.
The dead will rattle on. The world's designed
to have us rattle. So here, in hope and love,
some things I'd say if I were still alive
and if you asked, which obviously you have not.
And you have things to do. What we've got
is a great-grandfather with too much to say,
and great-grandchildren alive in their own day
and little channel between them. If you can listen
I'll try to make it not sound like a lesson.

A Story

When an act of kindness is not done
as it might have been done it doesn't behoove one
to fuss about it. As she who now would be
your great-great-great-grandmother put it to me
when I complained that my sister, who made it for love,
hadn't gotten the soup hot enough
(putting her arm around her granddaughter),
"Them that never goes to draw the water
won't ever leave the bucket in the well."

She could cipher some but she couldn't spell
past her own name.

I guess in the summer
when I turned twelve I left a wrench and a hammer
lying where I'd worked awhile on my bike.
I can hear the words that called me back
as if she had said them to me yesterday:
"The job ain't done till you put your tools away."

She taught me *hear* from *heed, poorly* from *sick,*
right from wrong, that couldn't read a lick.
I figured it out, though. If now she could not,
she knew how once but grew so old she forgot.
I wondered about the books she must have read
when she was young to carry in her head,
now that she was old, the things that she knew.
I looked in my dreams to find them. I still do.

Money

Money is flesh and bone. Honestly got,
money is one's own toil, time, and thought
in tangible form. Money unfairly had
is someone else's labor and should go bad
in any pocket or wallet or bank vault.
Should but doesn't. It isn't money's fault
if it doesn't care whose purse or pocket it fills.
It makes people agree and pays bill,
not knowing whether it was earned or won,
stolen or borrowed. It does what it's always done,
clamshells to plastic cards, a little better
for the creditor than for the debtor.

Buying and Selling

People have dangled like fish on hooks that were baited
by others who took their need to be inflated
and offered it back to them as promise and praise.
This can be done in a numberless number of ways—
by a shape in a bar that saw you come in alone,
a money-hunting voice on a telephone,
the people whose catalog you're amazed to get,
the woman trading you up to a bigger set,
just dollars more a month a few months longer.
Each one of these comprehends the hunger
to be someone deserving closer attention.
We comprehend it ourselves. It is ancient.
We could say, "We know your game," but then
we'd be confused, alone, and hungry again.
Part of what we pay, we pay for the car.
The rest we pay to be told who we are.

Truth and Truthfulness

Few things are more liberating to learn
than this: that when it's none of their concern
who ask you, "What do you do?" or "How much did you pay?"
it's not a lie, no matter what you say.
If they don't have any right to know,
tell them anything that isn't so.
In a lowered voice, it's like shelter and food
to nosy people and better than being rude.

Self-Control

Much comes out of the body and, by and large,
you'll be more comfortable if you're in charge,
deciding what and when the best you can,
and so will others be. There was a man
who never said a thing he didn't mean.
To him all mindless sounds were obscene,
and empty words especially profane,
signifying a failure in the brain.
He'd never said a word he had to regret.
The fact is, he was less likely to let
a rash or indeliberate word pass
than feel impromptu solid, liquid, or gas
part from his darkness in public, though anything wet
unbidden out of the body, even sweat,
left him perturbed and embarrassed profoundly. Hence,
he saw tears as a form of incontinence.
He nearly forgave the flesh its watery art;
worse were unmeasured words, the brain's fart.

He was a model of calm and eloquence,
a man of obvious breeding and good sense,
well known far beyond the neighborhood.
His children all left home as soon as they could.

Origami

It's wise to know one's self enough to share
a bed without embarrassment. Don't stare
too long at what you are. A woman once
was so concerned with how the psyche runs
she'd start to think a thought and watch the chain
of math and fire go skipping through her brain—
the silent explosions, the bright electric pools,
the spin and wobble of the molecules.
She watched herself watching herself reflect
till thought and thought began to intersect.
Whereupon
she folded into herself and she was gone.

Compassion

Have compassion for everyone you meet
even if they don't want it. What seems conceit,
bad manners, or cynicism is always a sign
of things no ears have heard, no eyes have seen.
You do not know what wars are going on
down there where the spirit meets the bone.

Agreeing

The flower is red, or yellow, as the case may be,
but you and everybody else agree
on which it is, and whose eyes are blue.
What does it mean that people agree with you?
There's no way that you can know you mean
the same color when two of you say, "Green,"
though colors, of course, are not what this is about.
No point in going on and spelling it out.

Caution

The odds can be terribly tempting. All the same,
be careful of the other person's game.
If someone offers you a deck of cards
and bets you anything the Jack of Hearts
will pop out and punch you in the nose,
sing "Moon River" and take off all his clothes,
then run around the room passing his hat,
don't take the bet. He'll do exactly that.

How It's Born in Us to Understand
That There Are Two Sides to Every Question

Think how we predators to every creature,
watching a TV show on the ways of nature,
a rabbit chased through snow by a beast of prey,
always root for the rabbit to get away.

War and Peace

Peace is something most often to be preferred
to confrontation for nations or lovers. The word
can be confusing, though, like a mockingbird.
You can hear it and not know what you've heard.
"Peace, at last!" you sigh. Which is to say
there won't be any violence today?
But there is the peace of death, of indifference,
of fear, of exhaustion, the peace of good sense,
and sometimes the peace of love. You'll want to find out
what peace it is before you spread it about.

Dust

There is a sadness so deep
the sun seems black
and you don't have to try to keep
the tears back

because you couldn't cry
if you wanted to.
Even your thoughts are dry.
All you can do

is stare at the ceiling
and wish the world would mend
and try to recall some better feeling
to no good end.

The Office Party

A monastery's careful austerity,
a mortuary's air of Gethsemane,
can only hint at the feel of the first few hours
back at work while memory churns and sours
after an office party that got too loose.
No glance was ever quicker or more abstruse
than those across the phones and keyboards
where people exchange their obligatory reports
with mumbling politeness and, meeting in doorways,
give way too far, step back with too much grace.
Some count their paper clips to break the spells
of those who whispered of meals and motels.

Beware of such a party and take care
that when a hand slides into underwear
the reasons it found its way last longer than all
the music and drinks and lapse of protocol.

God

Call evil all that debases the human spirit
for physical pleasure, for money, for power, for sport,
for simple convenience. Call a spirit debased
when someone has hurt a person or other beast
or the earth, its water, its air, the breathing plants,
without necessity and reverence.

Call what enriches the human spirit, good.

This will serve unless you say that God
has first to be written in as a Final Cause.
Fine, then. Say that God fashioned us all
after His image, that we are obliged by the Fall
to walk barefoot on the gravelly fields of faith
because we spoiled the spirit that was His breath.

But don't thank God for food, for bringing you through
the operation nearly as good as new,
for the tired swimmer safe, the soldier at ease.
You can't give God the credit for any of these
unless you hold Him accountable for the rest—
the mouth indifferent on the shrunken breast,
the soldier bagged, the swimmer in free fall,
the patient dead on the table. God did it all
or does nothing. To save a child from disease,
to bless a boat of ragbone refugees,
means choosing to turn from others, one by one.
God decides for all of us, or none.

Think, read, and pray, but there are only three
barely possible ways for God to be:

He may shape the fortunes of a few,
leaving the rest to falter or stumble through,
or He may plan it all, the watered shares,
the brakes in time, the toy at the top of the stairs.
But these are the same: if some are in His hands
then all are there, and neither law nor chance
is what we thought. Love, rage, neglect, or whim,
everything that happens falls to Him,
who keeps the carnal existence and the soul
of every person under His control,
stripping the flesh of one and stroking another.
No matter how much we believe the author
should love what is written down, who are we
to question how the universe should be?

Or say that He leaves us to chance and the love we find,
and takes no hand and possibly pays no mind.

Or say that He doesn't exist. Then what?

Think as we will of His nature or that He is not,
on what we believe about Him, in the end,
much more than our theologies depend.
Also most of politics, and much
of schoolroom and courtship and courtroom. The ways we touch.

whatever we believe affects all our actions –

Memory

You can't keep all of the past in a backpack or purse
all of the time. It's heavy, and what's worse,
it wouldn't leave room for much else,
what with drive-in movies, wooden motels,
a record player with needles, a touring car.
But what we were is much of what you are,
and what you are . . . believe me when I say
that what you are is going to wear away
little by little until, to your awful surprise,
you aren't all there; you barely recognize
what's left. Go now and rummage back to find
some odds and ends that may have been consigned
to dusty boxes somewhere in the mind.
Put them together and make of them a book
with ragged, bone-white leaves and a leather look.
Use whatever is there—how it was to spend
a long while in silence with a friend,
to watch the trembling death of a dog, to look
with wonder on the ordinary, to like
the feel in the flesh of time passing, to be
your crowded selves with nothing more from me.
I can't say what you'll find for stuff and glue.
I don't know all that you're made of. I hope you do.

Part 4: The Inaugural Poem, 1997

Of History and Hope

We have memorized America,
how it was born and who we have been and where.
In ceremonies and silence we say the words,
telling the stories, singing the old songs.
We like the places they take us. Mostly we do.
The great and all the anonymous dead are there.
We know the sound of all the sounds we brought.
The rich taste of it is on our tongues.
But where are we going to be, and why, and who? *central problem of poem —*
The disenfranchised dead want to know.
We mean to be the people we meant to be,
to keep on going where we meant to go.

But how do we fashion the future? Who can say how
except in the minds of those who will call it Now?
The children. The children. And how does our garden grow?
With waving hands—oh, rarely in a row—
and flowering faces. And brambles, that we can no longer allow.

Who were many people coming together / *nation + commerce at once*
cannot become one people falling apart.
Who dreamed for every child an even chance
cannot let luck alone turn doorknobs or not.
Whose law was never so much of the hand as the head *ACTIVE*
cannot let chaos make its way to the heart.
Who have seen learning struggle from teacher to child
cannot let ignorance spread itself like rot.
We know what we have done and what we have said,
and how we have grown, degree by slow degree,
believing ourselves toward all we have tried to become—
just and compassionate, equal, able, and free.

Gov = promote opp.

259

All this in the hands of children, eyes already set
on a land we never can visit—it isn't there yet—
but looking through their eyes, we can see
what our long gift to them may come to be.
If we can truly remember, they will not forget.

MOSES –
PROMISED
LAND

MEMORY =
OBTAINING FUTURE

260

New Poems

The Geography of Time

We think of time past
as the old country
where grandparents and parents came from.
We try to accord it, therefore, a kind of honor.
We set days aside in its name.
We speak with respect of those who have died there.

We care little, though,
for those who live there still,
or for anything left there.
"What does it matter?" we say,
"It's in the past,"
and tear off a calendar page
and answer the phone.
That leaves only the present and the future.

And we do believe in the present.
We pledge allegiance to it every day.

The future's another country,
one we're all being shuffled off to
like the long lines of losers
in some anonymous war,
never having seen anyone who has been there,
knowing nearly nothing about it,
not even the language,
not even the clothes to wear.

Love Poem with Toast

Some of what we do, we do
to make things happen,
the alarm to wake us up, the coffee to perc,
the car to start.

The rest of what we do, we do
trying to keep something from doing something,
the skin from aging, the hoe from rusting,
the truth from getting out.

With yes and no like the poles of a battery
powering our passage through the days,
we move, as we call it, forward,
wanting to be wanted,
wanting not to lose the rain forest,
wanting the water to boil,
wanting not to have cancer,
wanting to be home by dark,
wanting not to run out of gas,

as each of us wants the other
watching at the end,
as both want not to leave the other alone,
as wanting to love beyond this meat and bone,
we gaze across breakfast and pretend.

Talking to Himself
He Gets a Few Things Settled
in His Mind

What I hear mostly, sitting on this porch
every day from sundown, are the whining tires
of trucks on the bypass almost a mile away.
I guess there's no place in all America now
without the whine of tires. I can remember
when if you paid attention you could hear earthworms.

A few years ago, if someone had wanted to know
the difference in another place and this one,
I would have said it's tolerably close to the difference
between a kiss on the cheek and a kiss on the mouth.

Now people by the hundreds are moving here
to live where people are not coming in by the hundreds.

I can't die in the world that I was born in,
but few living now will do that,
what with all the leveling, the averaging out.
This is the way of more than human nature.

Talking about an aging universe,
an aging nation, whatever aging creature,
we mean differences slowly disappearing,
all extremes collapsing toward the center,
as sadness and joy commingle, and salt and sweet,
as intergalactic cold and the heat of the sun
will finally come together, and all the colors.

Think of speed and the speeding car as one,
of space and time falling into each other.
Think of Topeka, Kentucky. Des Moines, Texas.
That's all we really mean by getting old.

The truth of it, though, still does seem so unseemly
it makes the idea of dying go down easy,
which, committed as we are to dying,
serves a purpose. But everything serves a purpose.

I still can tell, if I listen very closely
between the 18-wheelers, the 26-wheelers,
a terrapin crossing the driveway, and one August night
an asteroid somewhere slamming into a planet.
If I can keep my hearing I'll be all right.

A Man in the Bar Says He Has Something to Say

There's something, sir, that somebody's going to tell you.
It might as well be me. About your woman.
I hope I don't get too far out of line
but you know how she is, how she can tease
to make you think she's going to tell you something
then leave you staring, feeling like a waiter
come back to take an order, the chairs empty,
napkins still wrapped around the silver.

You know how it is, how she opens her mouth
and winds her long hair around her fingers,
you waiting for words, she licking those pretty lips.

Remember when you ate supper alone
then watched a movie alone one Saturday night?
There wasn't a word of I'm sorry, I'll bet. I'll bet
she got undressed and said she'd tell you later.

Maybe that's what love is all about,
prologue and promise and then the screen goes black.

It isn't easy, is it, to pace and fret,
almost afraid of what she might blurt out,
almost afraid to see her coming back.

I'm going to tell you something you won't believe
and I'm not certain why I want to tell you.
It's not that I like you a lot or respect you much.
I'll sit and have a drink with you, though.
I've already told the waiter it's on my tab.
Now, hell, doesn't this beat all? Wouldn't you know?
I'll try to catch you later. That's my cab.

Unto One of the Least of These

With no one to talk to, he talked to the five fish
in a pond in the side yard in the shade of an oak—
Owen, Trudy, Trevor, Forrest, and Frederick,
the names beginning—this was his little joke—

the way the numbers one through five begin.
His wife had said he counted them every day
to see if the raccoon had eaten one.
He was only calling the roll. The fish had a way

of showing they knew he was there, the old preacher
come to share his parables again.
They took the bread he broke and never blinked,
no matter the stories he told, till he said, Amen.

If he immersed his fingers they nibbled the tips
but never allowed his hands to comfort and bless.
That was all right. People had done the same.
As if he were deaf, he listened to read their lips,
told them to go, baptized in the watery name,
and believed in the skulking raccoon less and less.

Thanatopsis

I got that title out of a book in school.
There was a poem about being dead.
"So live that when . . ." and so forth, sort of a rule
to keep bad things from finding a home in your head.

I ought to have paid more attention than I paid.
Tomorrow morning they're going to put that stuff
in one of my veins.

                I won't say I'm not afraid,
but take what I did, I guess it's fair enough.

Still, going where you've never gone before,
no matter who you knew that already went,
is tough. And I don't put a lot of store
in words that might not mean whatever they meant
in some dead language peasants heard them in.

Still, consequence—here's another good word—ensues
on every stumble some would call a sin.
Not little consequences. Not the blues.
I'm talking eternal pain or eternal blank.

We see others go and we think of ourselves and we're sad.
Some seemed to see something and didn't blink
at what they saw, so it might not be that bad.

Still, the screams in your dreams might be me.
Or then they might not. I could, in nothing flat,
go to nothing. But if hell means God has to be,
I'd find a sort of consolation in that.

For a Girl I Know about to Be a Woman

Because you'll find how hard it can be
to tell which part of your body sings,
you never should dally with any young man
who does any one of the following things:

tries to beat all the yellow lights;
says, "Big deal!" or "So what?"
more than seven times a day;
ignores yellow lines in a parking lot;

carries a radar detector;
asks what you did with another date;
has more than seven bumper stickers;
drinks beer early and whiskey late;

talks on a cellular phone at lunch;
tunes to radio talk shows;
doesn't fasten his seat belt;
knows more than God knows;

wants you to change how you do your hair;
spits in a polystyrene cup;
doesn't use his turn signal;
wants you to change your makeup;

calls your parents their given names;
doesn't know why you don't smoke;
has dirt under his fingernails;
makes a threat and calls it a joke;

pushes to get you to have one more;
seems to have trouble staying awake;
says "dago" and "wop" and words like that;
swerves a car to hit a snake;
sits at a table wearing a hat;
has a boneless handshake.

You're going to know soon enough
the ones who fail this little test.
Mark them off your list at once
and be very careful of all the rest.

Fifty

Year in, year out, most of us do our best
to make a hundred, perfect on the test.
The problems get harder, the teacher don't grade fair,
but hell, the bell ain't rung and you're halfway there.

Something to Believe In

For years, when things got tough, they looked to the day
when they would open the bottle of chardonnay
he'd bought beyond their means to show he cared,
and toast their love and their hope and the guts to stay.
The night they did it was no longer chardonnay.
Pouring it out they were sad and a little scared.

At Three Every Thursday Afternoon

Whatever it was gone wrong inside his head
that took him to the sessions he endured,
if he had meant to say, he never said.
After the doctor told him he was cured
they found him at home, hanging by a thread.

E-mail

She says good-bye, she's sorry, she's signing off.
She says it was all a mistake and there's nothing to say.
He guesses there isn't. He shuts down the computer
and listens to it putting things away.

First Date

He wanted so much to have it perfectly right,
him knowing what to do and her at ease,
he thought of nothing all week but Saturday night.

Then there they were, she pretty as you please,
he adroit and manful and grandly polite,
crossing every i and dotting the t's.

The Old Detective Begins His Last Interrogation
Looking for the Truth as Always

Son, I know what happened.
I just want to know
where the knife is.

Don't tell me there wasn't time.
There's always time.
Otherwise nothing at all could happen.
There are people who say
there isn't time in heaven.
If there were no time in heaven
how could new souls be taken in?
How could the saints converse?

Watch me wind my watch. What does that tell you?
God takes minutes like a secretary,
takes hours and years.
Why does He want them if there's no time in heaven?

And what about the music, the choirs of angels?
How can there be music if there's no time?

There's always time, son. Tell me about the knife.

The Longing

If I could have chosen another time to be
I'd blast off some centuries from now
to another populated galaxy.
It's a useless thought. I think it, anyhow,

the awkwardness in the beginning, trying to sense
what one is not supposed to see or say,
how to please, how not to give offense,
like in a nudist camp on the first day.

What kind of compliment can one pay,
fixing on their faces, maybe their hands?
Say "vanity" there and what does the word convey?
Connecting at a party, do they dance?

I like to think they would be amused and forgive
to see me trying so, with maybe a glance
at the dim star cluster where my people live,
the one I would have come from, given the chance.

Waking from a Dream

There was a nothingness, an impulse, a quark
flittering around existence in a place
of purest emptiness, no light, no dark,
a flicker of mathematics in manifold space,

less a movement than a moment. Still,
less a moment than numbers, that slowly start
folding into others the way they will,
like, say, on a checking account and a credit card.

Then moving to build toward everything we've been,
the quarks became the cores of electrons,
flying formations like clouds around their kin
who sit at the center of atoms like toy suns.

Already there were forces weak and strong,
the seeds of war and empire and molecules.
There were such clear signs all along
with no one to read them. Molecules in pools

complicated themselves into protoplasm
then suddenly into Mary Beth and Sam,
both looking dimly backward across a chasm
to numbers that somehow came to give a damn,

270

that one day would look an hour for a simile,
that one day would cry almost as one for the One
who might have been there when there was nowhere to be,
whose thought might be how universes run—

thoughts we perceive as shoestrings, crickets, and bread
and car keys and a maple leaf and a kiss.
So what is a thought? Better ask instead
what is not? Think of a thought as this:

A table. A dog. A door. A footstool. A fire.
And Sam and all his looks at Mary Beth. *LOVE - ABSTRACT THOUGHT*
Headaches and birthdays and glass. Failure and fear.
It isn't fact or fantasy. It's both. *REALITY FOR GOD*

Circling circles, I wonder why God should beguile
a thought of God into thinking I am me,
but this will do—you and some jazz a while
with a dog at your feet, or one that seems to be;

the senses of ourselves, of sense, of stuff;
the lifelong impression that we live;
what we have believed was wine; what feels like love;
your shapes I touch. These are convincing enough

to a man from a small town, not too quick,
who doesn't know a lot of arithmetic.

FOE RETREAT INTO COMMON MAN

Acknowledgments

Many of the poems in this book, sometimes in different versions, have appeared in the following publications: *American Literary Review, American Poetry Review, The American Scholar, Antaeus, The Antioch Review, Arkansas Times, The Barataria Review, Bits, Black Box, Boulevard, Brown Paper Bag, The Cal Creek Review, Chariton Review, The Cimarron Review, Concerning Poetry, Cornfield Review, Cotton Boll, CrazyHorse, Denver Quarterly, The Dickinson Review, Epos, The Falcon, Genesis West, The Georgia Review, The Ghent Quarterly, Image, Jeopardy, Kayak, The Laurel Review, Light Year, The Mediterranean Review, The Missouri Review, Motive, MSS, Negative Capability, New England Review, New England Review/Bread Loaf Quarterly, New Letters, New Orleans Review, North Dakota Quarterly, Northwest Review, Ohio Journal, The Pan American Review, Ploughshares, Poetry, Poetry Northwest, Poetry Now, Prairie Schooner, Red Weather, Saturday Review, Screen Actor News, Shenandoah, Southern Poetry Review, Sparrow, The Three Penny Review, Three Rivers Poetry Journal, Vanderbilt Review, The Virginia Quarterly Review, Voices, West Coast Poetry Review,* and *Yankee.*

Thanks to the editors of the following publications in which the listed poems appeared: *The Hudson Review* ("Clutter of Silence," "Lay of the Badde Wyf," "On the Sacrifice of a Siamese Twin at Birth," and "A Tenth Anniversary Photograph, 1952"); *The Kenyon Review* ("The Geography of Time," "Holiday Inn," "If Ever There Was One," "Listen," "Waking from a Dream," and "On Word That the Old Children's Stories Have Been Brought Up to Date"); *The Southern Review* ("Believing," "Ghosts," "Green Mansions," "A Lesson on the Twentieth Century," "Main Street," "Reading the Newspaper on Microfilm," "A Visitor's Guide to the Blue Planet," "Waiting for the Paper to Be Delivered," "The Well-Ordered Life," and "Why God Permits Evil").

Adjusting to the Light was published in 1992 by the University of Missouri Press, which has granted permission for poems from that collection to be included here. *A Circle of Stone* (1964), *Halfway from Hoxie* (rpt. 1977), *Why God Permits Evil* (1977), *Distractions* (1981), *The Boys on Their Bony Mules* (1983), *Imperfect Love* (1986), and *Living on the Surface* (1989) were all published by the Louisiana State University Press, which has also granted permission for poems from those collections to be included here.

And thank you Caroline Brt, David Baker, Jo McDougall, and Lothar Schäfer.

Index of Poem Titles

Illinois Poetry Series
Laurence Lieberman, Editor

History Is Your Own Heartbeat
Michael S. Harper (1971)

The Foreclosure
Richard Emil Braun (1972)

The Scrawny Sonnets and
Other Narratives
Robert Bagg (1973)

The Creation Frame
Phyllis Thompson (1973)

To All Appearances: Poems New
and Selected
Josephine Miles (1974)

The Black Hawk Songs
Michael Borich (1975)

Nightmare Begins Responsibility
Michael S. Harper (1975)

The Wichita Poems
Michael Van Walleghen (1975)

Images of Kin: New and
Selected Poems
Michael S. Harper (1977)

Poems of the Two Worlds
Frederick Morgan (1977)

Cumberland Station
Dave Smith (1977)

Tracking
Virginia R. Terris (1977)

Riversongs
Michael Anania (1978)

On Earth as It Is
Dan Masterson (1978)

Coming to Terms
Josephine Miles (1979)

Death Mother and Other Poems
Frederick Morgan (1979)

Goshawk, Antelope
Dave Smith (1979)

Local Men
James Whitehead (1979)

Searching the Drowned Man
Sydney Lea (1980)

With Akhmatova at the Black Gates
Stephen Berg (1981)

Dream Flights
Dave Smith (1981)

More Trouble with the Obvious
Michael Van Walleghen (1981)

The American Book of the Dead
Jim Barnes (1982)

The Floating Candles
Sydney Lea (1982)

Northbook
Frederick Morgan (1982)

Collected Poems, 1930–83
Josephine Miles (1983; reissue, 1999)

The River Painter
Emily Grosholz (1984)

Healing Song for the Inner Ear
Michael S. Harper (1984)

The Passion of the Right-Angled Man
T. R. Hummer (1984)

Dear John, Dear Coltrane
Michael S. Harper (1985)

Poems from the Sangamon
John Knoepfle (1985)

In It
Stephen Berg (1986)

The Ghosts of Who We Were
Phyllis Thompson (1986)

National Poetry Series

Eroding Witness
Nathaniel Mackey (1985)
Selected by Michael S. Harper

Palladium
Alice Fulton (1986)
Selected by Mark Strand

Cities in Motion
Sylvia Moss (1987)
Selected by Derek Walcott

The Hand of God and a Few
Bright Flowers
William Olsen (1988)
Selected by David Wagoner

The Great Bird of Love
Paul Zimmer (1989)
Selected by William Stafford

Stubborn
Roland Flint (1990)
Selected by Dave Smith

The Surface
Laura Mullen (1991)
Selected by C. K. Williams

The Dig
Lynn Emanuel (1992)
Selected by Gerald Stern

My Alexandria
Mark Doty (1993)
Selected by Philip Levine

The High Road to Taos
Martin Edmunds (1994)
Selected by Donald Hall

Theater of Animals
Samn Stockwell (1995)
Selected by Louise Glück

The Broken World
Marcus Cafagña (1996)
Selected by Yusef Komunyakaa

Nine Skies
A. V. Christie (1997)
Selected by Sandra McPherson

Lost Wax
Heather Ramsdell (1998)
Selected by James Tate

So Often the Pitcher Goes to Water
until It Breaks
Rigoberto González (1999)
Selected by Ai

Other Poetry Volumes

Local Men and *Domains*
James Whitehead (1987)

Her Soul beneath the Bone: Women's
Poetry on Breast Cancer
Edited by Leatrice Lifshitz (1988)

Days from a Dream Almanac
Dennis Tedlock (1990)

Working Classics: Poems on
Industrial Life
*Edited by Peter Oresick and
Nicholas Coles* (1990)

Hummers, Knucklers, and Slow
Curves: Contemporary Baseball
Poems
Edited by Don Johnson (1991)

Typeset in Utopia
with display in Triplex
Designed by Paula Newcomb
Composed at the University of Illinois Press
Manufactured by The Maple-Vail Book Manufacturing Group

TALKING TO ONE'S SELF → Sex 3

HUMAN FRAILTY 5 / → Love

SURVIVAL ◼

RELIGION 9
GOD

5 ↓ DEATH

Solitude of self /

WIFE IN THE POEMS

202 DEAF –
FRAILTY